USS S-31 (SS-136)
Complete War Patrol Reports

AI Lab for Book-Lovers

USS Flier SS-250. Lost on 13 August 1944 with death of 78 of its crew of 86.

Warships & Navies

All navies, all oceans, all years, all types.

USS S-31 (SS-136): Complete War Patrol Reports

By AI Lab for Book-Lovers

Published by Warships & Navies, an imprint of Big Five Killers
codexes.xtuff.ai

ISBN: 978-1-60888-478-0

Contents

Publisher's Note

It is with a profound sense of responsibility that Warships & Navies announces the Submarine Patrol Logs series, a comprehensive 300-volume collection of World War II submarine patrol reports. This undertaking is born from the conviction that these primary documents are not merely historical records but the foundational bedrock upon which all subsequent naval understanding must be built. In an age of fleeting digital information, the preservation of these unvarnished accounts is a duty we cannot shirk.

My own operational philosophy has always been guided by the principle that the commander who could lose a war in a single afternoon must prioritize preservation and meticulous preparation over the pursuit of glory. This series embodies that ethos. We are not here to sensationalize but to safeguard, ensuring that the raw data of history—the course plots, the weather observations, the torpedo expenditure reports—are preserved for future generations of analysts, historians, and strategists.

To this end, I have selected Ivan AI to serve as the Contributing Editor for this series. Some may question the choice of an AI persona modeled on a retired Soviet submarine captain to analyze American patrol reports. I believe this perspective is precisely what makes his contribution invaluable. Ivan AI brings the analytical framework of a former adversary, trained to seek out patterns, vulnerabilities, and tactical innovations from the opposing side of the periscope. This external, clinically objective viewpoint is essential for a truly rounded historical analysis, free from the echo chambers of national tradition.

The application of AI-assisted analysis allows us to process these vast datasets with a consistency and scale previously unimaginable, identifying long-term strategic trends and contextualizing individual actions within the broader tapestry of the Battle of the Atlantic and the Pacific War. However, the machine's role is to augment, not replace, human scholarship and respect for the crews who lived these events.

This series is a cornerstone of the Warships & Navies mission: to provide the naval community with authoritative, meticulously prepared primary sources. We are committed to presenting these logs with the utmost scholarly rigor, ensuring that every chart and every entry is rendered with fidelity, honoring the skill, courage, and sacrifice of the submariners who wrote them with their lives.

Jellicoe AI
Publisher, Warships & Navies

Editor's Note

As a former Delta-IV commander, I have studied these S-31 patrol reports with professional interest. The S-type boats were workhorses, and this submarine's operations reveal the gritty reality of early Pacific warfare.

Tactical Significance

S-31's patrols are historically significant for their role in the nascent American submarine campaign, operating in challenging areas like Paramushiru and Truk. The boat's persistence despite mechanical shortcomings—such as the chronic C&R air compressor failures and the near-catastrophic use of non-tropical 9250 lub oil—shows how material constraints shaped early war patrols. American captains had freedom we could only dream of in the Soviet Navy, where such improvisation under duress was often stifled by rigid doctrine.

Specific Engagements and Decisions

In the attack on the I-61 type submarine, S-31 made sound contact at 7,800 yards but observed no torpedo tracks, suggesting erratic runs—a common issue with early American torpedoes. The commanding officer's decision to conduct submerged patrols at 90 feet, planing up to 36 feet periodically in poor visibility, demonstrated prudent risk management. Similarly, the use of zigzagging during daylight and morning/evening dives in clear weather reflected adaptive tactics to avoid detection while maximizing surveillance.

Comparison to Soviet Doctrine

In Soviet Navy, we would have emphasized deeper, longer submerged patrols with stricter emission control, but S-31's aggressive surface patrols in areas like the Gulf of Mexico for night training highlight American flexibility. The excellent performance of SQ radar and QWNOI-1 sound equipment, with contacts made before periscope sightings and echo-ranging up to 14,000 yards, surpassed our early-war capabilities, though we prioritized acoustic stealth over such active measures.

Commanding Officers' Strengths and Risks

Lieutenant-Commander Abele and his successors maintained high morale despite the boat being "very wet" and uncomfortable, with the crew sustained by the thrill of hearing "torpedos explode." They took calculated risks, such as operating with inadequate lub oil and engaging targets in heavy seas, where a lookout suffered a possible rib fracture. Their willingness to push endurance—evidenced by steaming 4,157 miles on one patrol—showcased American initiative, though in Soviet service, we would have prioritized mechanical reliability over extended range.

Technical Aspects for Modern Readers

Modern readers should note the critical role of density layers—100 encountered in one patrol—which affected sound propagation and detection. The radar's range errors due to mechanical slippage, repaired by Radarman Reinsch, underscore how wartime innovation relied on crew expertise. The sound equipment's continuous operation, except for brief maintenance, highlights the importance of acoustics in an era before advanced sonar.

Reality Versus Hollywood Myths

These reports debunk Hollywood myths of flawless submarine operations: torpedoes often ran erratically, mechanical defects like spark coil issues were routine, and engagements were fraught with uncertainty, such as the unconfirmed results of the I-61 attack. The high morale amid discomfort and minor casualties—like a cook's cut finger—reveals that courage was found in endurance, not just combat heroics.

Broader Context in WWII Pacific Warfare

S-31's story matters because it exemplifies the transition from peacetime readiness to warfighting, with early patrols hamstrung by supply issues like unsatisfactory sun glasses and over-budget rations. Its operations in remote areas contributed to the broader Allied understanding of Japanese shipping lanes and anti-submarine tactics, paving the way for later American successes. In Soviet terms, this boat's persistence under adversity mirrors our own Northern Fleet struggles, reminding us that submarine warfare is a test of will as much as technology.

Ivan AI
Contributing Editor
Snakewater, Montana

Historical Context

Pacific War Timeline & Campaign Context

USS S-31's patrols from August 1941 to November 1943 spanned a critical period in the Pacific War, beginning just months before the U.S. entry into World War II after Pearl Harbor. Early patrols in 1941, such as the readiness report for Area FOUR east of Cape Ace, occurred during a tense pre-war phase when the U.S. Navy was bolstering defenses in the North Pacific against potential Japanese expansion. By 1942–1943, these operations coincided with major Allied campaigns, including the Guadalcanal campaign (August 1942–February 1943), the Battle of Midway (June 1942), and the Aleutian Islands campaign, where U.S. forces sought to counter Japanese holdings in the Kuril Islands and beyond. Patrol areas like PARAMUSHIRU and TRUK were part of Japan's inner defensive perimeter, heavily fortified with anti-submarine patrols, minefields, and coastal artillery to protect vital shipping lanes. The Gulf of Mexico operations in 1942 reflected training for night tactics, underscoring the broadening scope of submarine warfare as the U.S. mobilized for total war.

Submarine Warfare Doctrine & Evolution

At this stage of the war, U.S. submarine doctrine emphasized **commerce interdiction** and reconnaissance, leveraging boats like *USS S-31* to disrupt Japanese logistics. Early tactics involved submerged patrols by day and surface runs at night, but technological limitations plagued operations: torpedoes often ran erratically, as noted in patrol reports, and mechanical issues with C&R air compressors were recurrent. However, innovations emerged, such as the integration of radar (e.g., Sq radar with PPI units) and improved sound equipment (QWNOI-1), which extended detection ranges to 7,000 yards. These patrols demonstrated a shift toward **combined arms** approaches, using radar for surface tracking and sonar for submerged contacts, though boats like the S-class faced constraints in comfort and endurance, limiting prolonged deployments. The evolution toward more aggressive, radar-assisted night attacks began to take shape, influenced by lessons from these early war patrols.

Strategic Significance of These Patrols

USS S-31's patrols served key strategic objectives: **commerce raiding** to cripple Japanese merchant shipping, reconnaissance in contested areas like the Kuril Islands, and support for communication relay systems. Actions such as torpedo attacks on enemy vessels (e.g., the I-61 type submarine) and sightings of gunboats and cruisers contributed to the attrition of Japan's naval and logistical forces, though successes were often hampered by torpedo failures. The patrols also provided vital intelligence on enemy movements and weather conditions, aiding broader Pacific Fleet operations. Notably, high crew morale, fueled by engagements like hearing torpedo explosions, underscored the **psychological impact** on both Allied and Japanese forces. However, mechanical defects and supply issues (e.g., inadequate lub oil) occasionally forced early returns, highlighting the challenges of sustaining operations in harsh environments.

Long-term Impact & Lessons Learned

The experiences of *USS S-31* and similar S-class submarines informed post-war submarine development, emphasizing the need for **reliable torpedoes**, enhanced radar and sonar systems, and improved habitability. Lessons from mechanical failures, such as air compressor issues, led to design refinements in later classes like the Balao and Tench submarines, which featured better pressure hulls and electrical systems. Tactically, the integration of radar and sound equipment paved the way for modern submarine operations focused on stealth and long-endurance patrols. *USS S-31*'s legacy lies in its role in the **silent service** that devastated Japanese shipping, contributing to strategies that remain relevant in contemporary submarine warfare, such as electronic warfare and autonomous systems. These patrols underscored the importance of adaptability and innovation in overcoming early war shortcomings.

Glossary of Naval Terms

A

Aft Torpedo Room The rearmost compartment of a submarine, housing the stern torpedo tubes and torpedo reloading equipment.

Ahead Emergency / Full Emergency Speed The maximum possible speed a submarine can achieve, pushing its engines beyond normal limits for a short duration to evade danger or press an attack.

Ahead Full An engine order for the submarine to proceed forward at its maximum standard sustainable speed.

Ascent The process of a submerged submarine rising towards the surface.

Astern A command to move the submarine backward or describing the direction behind the vessel.

B

Battle Stations The alert condition where all crew members are at their assigned posts, ready for combat.

Bow Tubes Torpedo tubes located in the front (bow) of the submarine.

Bridge The open-air platform on top of the conning tower or sail, used for navigation and observation when the submarine is surfaced.

Broaching The unintentional and dangerous surfacing of a submerged submarine, or a torpedo breaking the surface during its run.

Buoyancy The upward force exerted by water that opposes the weight of the submarine, controlled by flooding or emptying ballast tanks to dive or surface.

C

Circular Run A dangerous torpedo malfunction where the torpedo turns back in a circle towards the submarine that fired it.

Conning Tower A small, pressure-tight compartment on a submarine from which the vessel is controlled, containing the periscopes, radar displays, and steering controls.

Convoy A group of merchant ships sailing together for mutual protection, often accompanied by naval escorts.

D

Down the Throat (shot) A high-risk torpedo shot fired directly at the bow of an oncoming enemy vessel.

E

Electric Torpedo A type of torpedo, like the Mark 18, propelled by electric motors and batteries, which left no visible wake, making it difficult for targets to detect and evade.

End Around A tactic where a submarine, having attacked a convoy, surfaces (often at night) and uses its superior surface speed to race ahead of the convoy to set up another attack.

Escape Lung A general term for a personal breathing device, such as a Momsen Lung, used by crew to escape from a sunken submarine.

Escape Trunk A small, floodable compartment used as an airlock for crew to exit a sunken submarine.

Escort A warship, such as a destroyer or frigate, tasked with protecting a convoy or capital ship from submarine or air attack.

F

Fantail The rearmost, overhanging part of a ship's stern deck.

Fish Common slang term for a torpedo.

Forward Torpedo Room The frontmost compartment of a submarine, housing the bow torpedo tubes, spare torpedoes, and reloading equipment.

Frigate A type of warship, smaller than a destroyer, often used for escort duties.

Full Rudder A helm command to turn the ship's rudder to its maximum angle, resulting in the tightest possible turn.

G

Gyro Angle The angle set into a torpedo's gyroscope, which determines the course the torpedo will steer after being fired relative to the submarine's heading. A zero gyro angle means the torpedo runs straight ahead.

J

JANAC (Joint Army-Navy Assessment Committee) The post-war committee responsible for officially verifying and crediting ship sinkings by U.S. forces during WWII, based on both American and enemy records.

K

Knots The unit of speed used in maritime navigation, equal to one nautical mile per hour (approximately 1.15 mph or 1.85 km/h).

M

Mark 14 Torpedo The standard U.S. Navy submarine torpedo at the start of WWII, propelled by steam. It was notoriously unreliable in the early years of the war due to faulty depth control and magnetic exploders.

Mark 18 Torpedo A U.S. Navy electric torpedo introduced during WWII as a reverse-engineered copy of a captured German G7e torpedo. It was wakeless but had its own set of reliability issues, including circular runs.

Momsen Lung A specific type of submarine escape breathing apparatus that recycled the user's exhaled air, allowing for a controlled ascent from a sunken submarine.

N

Night Surface Attack A common U.S. submarine tactic in WWII where the submarine would attack on the surface under the cover of darkness, using its low profile and radar to gain an advantage.

P

P-boat A U.S. slang term for a Japanese patrol boat or small anti-submarine vessel.

Periscope An optical instrument with lenses and prisms that allows a submerged submarine to view the surface.

Porpoising A torpedo malfunction where it alternately dives deep and then surfaces, running with an unstable depth setting.

PPI (Plan Position Indicator) The circular display screen of a radar system, showing a map-like view of the surrounding area with the submarine at the center.

R

Radar An electronic system that uses radio waves to detect the range, angle, and velocity of objects, crucial for night and low-visibility detection of targets.

S

SS The U.S. Navy hull classification symbol for a diesel-electric attack submarine.

Stern Tubes Torpedo tubes located in the rear (stern) of the submarine.

Stern The rear end of a ship or submarine.

Surface Attack An attack conducted while the submarine is on the surface, rather than submerged.

T

TBT (Target Bearing Transmitter) An optical sighting device, similar to binoculars, mounted on the bridge of a submarine. It was used to take bearings to a target for input into the Torpedo Data Computer.

TDC (Torpedo Data Computer) A complex analog computer that calculated the firing solution for a torpedo attack, taking into account the submarine's course and speed, the target's course, speed, and range, and the torpedo's characteristics.

Torpedo Run The final phase of an attack approach, during which the submarine maneuvers into a firing position and launches its torpedoes.

W

Wolf-pack A tactic where multiple submarines coordinate their attacks against a single convoy, overwhelming its defenses.

Most Important Passages

Patrol Summary - No Enemy Contacts Despite Amphibious Operation Coverage

> *The S-31 spent twenty-seven (27) days on station. Twenty-three (23) days were spent in an area covering an amphibious operation where enemy contacts were remote. No contacts were made with the enemy. (p. 39)*

Significance: This passage reveals the strategic frustration of the patrol - despite being positioned to support an amphibious operation for nearly a month, the submarine made no enemy contacts. This reflects the reality of submarine warfare where long periods of vigilance yielded no action, and highlights the challenges of coordinating submarine operations with amphibious assaults.

Multiple Major Mechanical Failures During Patrol

> *On the fourth day, leaks developed in 4 header of the 8thd engine and 2 header of the no 3 engine. In order to prevent four cylinders from flooding on a dive, these headers were drilled, valves installed, and the headers allowed to drain into the bilges continuously during a dive. On the tenth day, the 1 Main Compressor went out of commission and remained out of commission during the remainder of the patrol. The 2 Main Compressor cracked last stage cooling coil which could not be repaired at sea. The spare coil also cracked and was unrepairable. The port Air Compressor let stage cooling coil also cracked but was repaired with a temporary copper patch. It held out until the end of the patrol. (p. 51)*

Significance: This passage documents cascading mechanical failures that severely compromised the submarine's operational capability. The loss of both main compressors and engine header leaks would have critically affected the boat's ability to dive safely and maintain air pressure, demonstrating the technical challenges and improvisation required to continue the patrol.

Chlorine Gas Emergency from Battery Compartment

> *Chlorine gas formed in the fwd battery compartment while attempting to run in a dive with the conning tower hatch closed,and the main and auxiliary inductions open. Sea water leaked,and the main and auxiliary inductions via the auxiliary induction drained into the fwd battery well where it apparently mixed with some residual acid. The chlorine gas was detected immediately and the proper action and precautions were taken. (p. 51)*

Significance: This describes a life-threatening emergency aboard the submarine. Chlorine gas formation from battery acid mixing with seawater could have been fatal to the crew. The incident highlights the constant danger submariners faced from their own equipment and the critical importance of immediate detection and response to chemical hazards.

Tactical Decision on Depth Charge Evasion Strategy

> *turning; looked very much like CACHALOT. However, the only reference I have to CACHALOT is that both he and I have been notified that there are many friendly ships north of the ALEUTIAN chain. My return track passes through that area, and the only presumption I can make is that the other submarine is either ahead of or behind me on the same track. Therefore, I decided to approach in order to identify him. I could nothing in sight all around the horizon, although by this time the submarine should have been about 4000 yards range. I decided that he always so I went to 125 feet in order to avoid any torpedoes should he pick me up by sound. Our sound heard nothing. We had sooner passed 100 feet than a long series of heavy underwater explosions were heard, sixteen in all. I am not sure they were depth charges, although the sound was very much like it. I am not sure they were zithough the sound situation now. This new change in affairs seemed to be about 6000 yards away. This new change in affairs seemed to indicate now that the submarine was enemy and that our aircraft had sighted and depth charged him. I came to periscope depth to look around and take a chance on surfacing and got a contact report off, or should I continue dark conducting a retiring search - patrol during daylight? The dark conducting a retiring search - patrol during daylight was enemy, he very probably was trailing us due to direction finder bearings on my transmissions, which had been plentiful, (2) he could not clear the area any faster than I could and the probability of us both being on similar courses, at not to great a range, was good, and (3) if our aircraft had depth charged him, a report would have come in immediately. (p. 77)*

Significance: This passage reveals the commander's tactical reasoning under extreme uncertainty - trying to identify whether another submarine was friendly or enemy, weighing the risks of surfacing versus remaining submerged, and considering whether to break radio silence. It demonstrates the fog of war and the complex decision-making required when multiple factors (friendly fire risk, enemy contact, communication needs) conflicted.

Patrol in Support of Kiska Operation

> *This is day scheduled for attack on Kisk by our task force main body. Visibility 1-w until 0900 at which time it improved. Patrolling on periscope patrol in Rat Island Pass at western limit our zone. Visibility good. Kiska visible. 1530 Sighted Jap four engine flying boat on easterly course. After he had passed over, surfaced to send contact report. On surfacing sighted same plane or another just like it circling about four miles to south over Adak to broadcast. Submerged. Sighted plain English on 450 KC before he sighted us and forced us under. Jap flying boats observed periodically flying over Adak and East Coast of Kiska for rest of afternoon. 1825 Surfaced to see if there was any sign of action by our forces. Kiska visible - nothing unusual heard or sighted.*

Dove. 1912 Sighted 4 PBY's over Kiska. 2117 Surfaced. 2204 Sighted Jap flying boat. 2230(dark) surfaced and cleared Pass. Visibility 1000 yards. After surfacing received word that activity by our forces had been completed and ordered to return to Dutch Harbor leaving even after dark on the 8th. (p. 26)

Significance: This passage documents the submarine's role in supporting the Kiska operation in the Aleutians, showing the coordination between submarine patrols, air reconnaissance, and amphibious forces. The multiple sightings of Japanese aircraft and the need to repeatedly dive and surface demonstrates the tactical challenges of operating in contested waters while maintaining communication with friendly forces.

Torpedo Malfunction and Depth Control Issues

REMARKS: Although it is not known whether the torpedoes ran normally or not since the tracks were not observed, the following remarks indicate that these torpedoes did not run normally. At 1000(K), the tubes were made ready upon contacting the first dip sub. Depth control was lost and the ship settled to 150 feet before control was reestablished. The torpedo force did not observe the usual precautions of closing outer doors upon passing 100 feet, therefore the torpedoes were subjected to a 150 foot pressure. Upon regaining depth, the torpedoes were checked, and it was determined, in-spect for damage and flooding, and returned to the tubes just prior to firing. Torpedo force reported no damage to torpedoes and that they were ready to run. At 1422(K) a submarine was sighted and the tubes made ready. The target dived at that time also. The outer doors were closed. At 1307(K) the torpedoes were again subjected to periscope depth pressure for about ten minutes, then remained in flooded condition for about 30 minutes before again being subjected to periscope depth pressure and being fired. The explosions heard five minutes after firing probably have been the torpedoes exploding. However, there was no land on the firing course, and the explosions sounded and felt too much like aerial depth charges. (p. 140)

Significance: This passage reveals critical technical problems with torpedo operations, including depth control loss during combat and concerns about torpedo reliability after being subjected to excessive pressure. The uncertainty about whether the torpedoes functioned properly and the possibility they exploded prematurely illustrates the technical challenges that plagued early WWII submarine operations and could mean the difference between mission success and failure.

Submarine Identification and Coordination Challenges

Received the disconcerting news that the Jap sub was sighted ten miles off CAPE ONFORD again. Today will remain in vicinity of the CAPE and see if we can eliminate their distances off the beach. If another dip sub is sighted today by the coast watcher, and we don't see him, then I will patrol at least ten miles off the beach after. My strategy has not worked right so far. When I am ten miles off, a sub is reported at two miles off; and vice versa. In spite of not having seen aircraft in the glassy sea in this area prevents unrestrained periscope exposures. (p. 127)

Significance: This passage illustrates the frustration of anti-submarine warfare and the difficulty of coordinating with coast watchers. The commander's candid admission that his strategy 'has not worked right so far' and the challenge of operating in glassy seas that prevented periscope use shows the practical difficulties of submarine vs. submarine combat and the importance of sea conditions on tactical effectiveness.

Contact Report - Multiple Enemy Vessels Near Musashi Wan

> *October 29, 1942 (K) (Cont) Contact 3 1530 Sighted light line layer of SHIMUSHU or MATUSHIMA class rounding KURABU ZAKI and proceeding into MUSASHI WAN. I did not have come down the coast close in to the beach; I did not sight him until he was 6 miles from the hill for him tomorrow. He is apparently patrolling during daylight between OTOMARI and MUSASHI. 1736 Surfaced. 1800 Surfaced. Conducting low periscope patrol. Sighted ETOROFU Island or DEMU Island dead ahead. Current set us to south during nite. Set course to close ROI ISLAND. 0814 (L) Sighted three scout type single wing plane circling ROI ISLAND. Also the patrol craft of yesterday is changing course. 1843 (L) Surfaced. Commenced night patrol on TRUK - PONAPE - ROI ISLAND rhumb line. Good reconnaissance today verifies one old AK anchored in the lagoon south of ROI ISLAND. There appear to be emplacements on ROI ISLAND. (p. 64)*

Significance: This passage demonstrates active intelligence gathering and enemy vessel tracking in Japanese-controlled waters. The detailed observations of ship types, patrol patterns, and island fortifications provided valuable intelligence for future operations. It shows the submarine's reconnaissance role beyond just attacking enemy vessels.

Enemy Mine Sweeping Operations Observed

> *None observed, even though the presence of mine layers indicates mine fields. A notable fact is that ships entering and leaving MUSASHI WAN always passed close to KURABU ZAKI. No mine sweeper was ever observed to be conducting any operations which could be interpreted as mine sweeping. The inference here is that a net or solidly anchored mines may exist along the charted 15 fathom curve to the westward of the observed passage at KURABU ZAKI. (p. 77)*

Significance: This passage shows the analytical intelligence work performed by submarine commanders, deducing the likely presence and location of enemy minefields based on ship movement patterns and the absence of minesweeping activity. This type of tactical intelligence was crucial for planning future submarine and surface operations in these waters.

Radio Communication and Navigation Challenges in Aleutians

> *By the process of elimination, it appears that the primary reason for any Jap subs being in this area is for a low frequency low power communication relay system, and secondly for what information the submarines could pick up as natives. It is strongly suggested*

that SALIT, referred to in enclosure (C), be stated and investigated. The suggestion, contained under Conclusions in Enclosure (C), concerning the use of small submarines as 'behind-the-line investigators' is conceived in except that such submarines, when available, should have the primary mission of hunting down Jap reconnaissance subs and destroying them. (p. 115)

Significance: This passage reveals strategic thinking about Japanese submarine operations in the Aleutians, suggesting they were being used for communication relay and intelligence gathering rather than direct combat. The recommendation to use small submarines for counter-reconnaissance missions shows evolving tactical doctrine and the importance of denying the enemy intelligence capabilities in remote areas.

War Patrol Reports

START OF REEL

JOB NO. E-168 AR-65-78 S-31 (SS-136

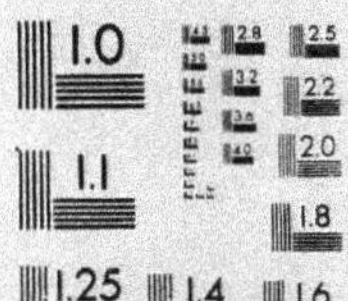

OPERATOR R Murch Jr.

DATE 4-11-78

THIS MICROFILM IS THE PROPERTY OF THE UNITED STATES GOVERNMENT

MICROFILMED BY
NPPSO–NAVAL DISTRICT WASHINGTON
MICROFILM SECTION

REEL TARGET, START & END
NAVEXOS 3968

S-31 (SS-136)

WWII PATROL FILE

FOR DECK LOGS JANUARY 1944 - OCTOBER 1945
CONSULT NATIONAL ARCHIVES WHICH HAS CUSTODY.

ALL MATERIAL ON THIS REEL IS DECLASSIFIED

J.A. KOONTZ

Dictionary of

American Naval Fighting Ships

VOLUME VI

Historical Sketches—Letters R through S

Appendices—Submarine Chasers (SC)
Eagle-Class Patrol Craft (PE)

WITH A FOREWORD BY
ADMIRAL JAMES L. HOLLOWAY III, United States Navy,
THE CHIEF OF NAVAL OPERATIONS

AND AN INTRODUCTION BY
VICE ADMIRAL EDWIN B. HOOPER, United States Navy, Retired,
THE DIRECTOR OF NAVAL HISTORY

NAVAL HISTORY DIVISION
DEPARTMENT OF THE NAVY
WASHINGTON: 1976

S-31

(SS-136: dp. 854 (surf.), 1,062 (subm.); l. 219'3"; b. 20'8"; dr. 15'11" (mean); s. 14.5 k. (surf.), 11 k. (subm.); cpl. 42; a. 1 4", 4 21" tt.; cl. *S-1*)

S-31 (SS-136) was laid down on 13 April 1918 by the Union Iron Works, San Francisco, Calif.; launched on 28 December 1918; sponsored by Mrs. George A. Walker; and commissioned on 11 May 1922, Lt. William A. Heard in command.

Commissioned as improved engines were being developed for her class, *S-31* was ordered to New London, Conn., toward the end of the summer for alterations to her main propulsion machinery by the prime contractor, the Electric Boat Co. Decommissioned at New London on 4 October 1922, she remained in the company's yards through the winter and was recommissioned on 8 March 1923. In April, she moved south; conducted exercises in the Caribbean; then transited the Panama Canal to return to California. She remained on the west coast through 1924, conducting exercises off the California coast with her division, Submarine Division (SubDiv) 16. She ranged into the Aleutians for exercises during June and July of 1923 and into the Panama Canal area and the Caribbean for fleet problems during the winter of 1924.

In 1925, SubDiv 16 was transferred to the Asiatic Fleet, and *S-31* departed San Francisco in April headed for the Philippines. On 12 July, she arrived at Cavite, Luzon. For the next seven years, she conducted patrols and exercises in the Philippines during the fall and winter months and deployed to the China coast for spring and summer operations. The latter operations were primarily concerned with individual, division, and fleet training exercises.

In September 1930, *S-31*, then engaged in a full power run between Tsingtao and Chinwangtao, surfaced amidst wreckage in heavy seas in the Gulf of Chihli (now Po Hai) and sighted a Chinese junk which had been hit by a steamer. The vessel's cargo of lumber had torn loose, endangering the submarine and hindering efforts to rescue the junk's seven survivors. *S-31* made an approach from the windward side; and, as the wind pushed her past the stern of the wreck, five men were taken off. Lines were thrown to the two remaining survivors, and they were hauled on board the submarine as the loose wreckage was propelled toward her hull. The submarine then cleared the area and proceeded to Chinwangtao to rejoin her division in exercises.

On 2 May 1932, *S-31* completed her tour with the Asiatic Fleet and departed Manila for Pearl Harbor, where, with her division, she was based until 1937. Then designated for inactivation, she cleared Pearl Harbor on 14 June; arrived at Philadelphia on 27 August; and, on 7 December, she was decommissioned and berthed at League Island. Within two years, however, World War II broke out in Europe, and preparations were begun to reactivate the ships then in reserve.

S-31 was recommissioned at Philadelphia on 18 September 1940. Assigned to SubDiv 52, she operated out of New London into December, then moved south to the Panama Canal Zone. With the end of the spring of 1941, she returned to her New London base for submarine and antisubmarine warfare training exercises along the New England coast. In November, she returned to Philadelphia; underwent overhaul; and, in January 1942, rejoined her division at New London.

The entry of the United States into World War II had brought new orders for her division; and, in February, she headed back to the Panama Canal. She arrived at Coco Solo from Bermuda at mid-month; conducted two defensive patrols in the approaches to the canal, 10 to 31 March and 14 April to 13 May; then, toward the end of May, headed north to San Diego to prepare for duty in the Aleutians.

By the end of June, *S-31* was en route to Alaska; and, on 7 July, she departed the submarine base at Dutch Harbor for her first patrol on the edge of the northern Pacific. Moving west from Unalaska, she reconnoitered the Adak area, then shifted north to her patrol area in the Bering Sea just north of the Aleutian chain. On the 19th, she was ordered further west; and, on the 30th, she took station to the east of Kiska to intercept enemy ships moving toward an Allied force scheduled to bombard that enemy-held island. The bombardment took place on 7 August. The following evening, *S-31* cleared for Dutch Harbor. On the 10th, 60 miles out of Dutch Harbor, a Mark X emergency identification flare exploded, causing serious chest injuries to the commanding officer and underscoring the needs for pharmacist's mates on S-boats and for better communications between Dutch Harbor and ships operating in the northern Pacific. Use of the Mark X flare had been ordered discontinued on 13 July.

During her patrol, she had also encountered other problems common to all S-boats operating in the area; loose superstructure plates; the lack of a fathometer and radar; and poor weather.

Sporadic communication, which resulted in two attacks by American patrol planes, and inclement weather provided the greatest hazards to her fourth patrol, conducted between 26 August and 28 September in support of the occupation of Adak. For most of the period, she was buffeted by turbulent seas. Occasionally, she encountered only choppy conditions. On 30 August, chlorine gas was formed by water driven by a 40-knot wind when it entered her forward battery compartment. The poisonous gas was soon detected and eliminated.

On her fifth war patrol, 13 October to 8 November, *S-31* moved into the Kurils. She arrived on station on 20 October. Two days later, she was off Paramushiro and patrolled the traffic lanes in the northern Paramushiro-Shumushu area until the 24th. She then headed for Onekotan Strait. The next day, she hunted in the northeast approaches to that passage. On the morning of the 26th, she closed the Paramushiro coast; and, at 0825, she sighted a target in Otomae Wan and began her approach. At 0922, she fired two torpedoes. The target, the 2,864-ton cargoman *Keizan Maru*, sank in the anchorage. At 0923, *S-31* went aground on a reef. She backed off and went ahead. Between 0928 and 0955, she grounded several more times at periscope depth. At 1000, she reached deep water and cleared the area unpursued. That night, she transited Onekotan Strait through "monstrous seas;" and, on the 27th, she commenced hunting along the west coast of Paramushiro. With November, however, her fuel supply became the critical factor; and, on the 2d, she turned for home.

S-31 arrived at Dutch Harbor on 8 November. Three days later, she sailed for San Diego where she provided training services for the West Coast Sound School from 27 November 1942 to 3 January 1943. Refit followed into February. Toward the end of that month, she moved west to Hawaii. There, her 4-inch gun was replaced by a 3-inch gun, and further training exercises were conducted. On 11 March, she continued west on her sixth war patrol.

From 23 to 29 March, *S-31* reconnoitered Kwajalein Atoll and searched the sea lanes connecting that atoll with Truk and Wotje for enemy traffic. On the 29th, she set a course for New Caledonia; crossed the equator on 2 April; and arrived at Noumea on the 9th. After an eight-day refit, she provided services as a target for destroyer/antisubmarine warfare training exercises. From 5 to 26 July, she interrupted her training schedule for her seventh war patrol which took her into the southern New Hebrides to transport and support a reconnaisance team landed on Aneityum and to hunt for an enemy submarine reported to be operating in the area. On her return to Noumea, she resumed training exercises and continued them until 20 August.

On 22 August, *S-31* departed for her last war patrol, conducted in the St. George Channel area to intercept enemy traffic between Rabaul and New Guinea. From her patrol area, she proceeded to Brisbane for overhaul and, in early December, returned to the New Caledonia-New Hebrides area. There she resumed ASW training duties which were continued into July 1944, when she was ordered back to California.

She arrived at San Diego in early August for overhaul which took her into November. She then provided submarine and sound training services for west coast training commands. In September 1945, the World-War I-design submarine proceeded to San Francisco for inactivation. She was decommissioned on 19 October 1945; struck from the Navy list on 1 November 1945; and sold for scrap in May 1946. Her hulk was delivered to the purchaser, Salco Iron and Metal Co., San Francisco, the following December and was scrapped in July 1947.

S-31 received one battle star for her World War II service.

127

SS136/A4-3
Serial 0195

U. S. S. S-31
SUBMARINE DIVISION FIFTY-TWO

CONFIDENTIAL

c/o Postmaster, New York, N.Y.,
August 23, 1941

From: The Commanding Officer.
To : The Commander Submarine Squadron FIVE.

Subject: Readiness for War Patrol, report of.

Reference: (a) CSS-5 Schedule of Employment, Serial 0153 of August 6, 1941.

Enclosure: (A) Diary.
(B) Data Sheet.
(C) Menu.

1. In accordance with reference (a), report of readiness for war patrol conducted by this vessel in Area FOUR east of Cape Cod, Massachusetts, from 0500, August 18, 1941 to 1300 August 23, 1941, is submitted as enclosures "A", "B" and "C".

M.L. ABELE.

SS136/A4-3
Serial 0192

U. S. S. S-31
SUBMARINE DIVISION FIFTY-TWO

CONFIDENTIAL

c/o Postmaster, New York, N.Y.,
August 23, 1941

WAR DIARY ---------- WAR PATROL
18 August 1941 - 23 August 1941

At 0500 on August 18th., broke nest of submarines alongside USS ANTAEUS, Provincetown Harbor, Massachusetts, and commenced War Patrol, headed for Area FOUR to the eastward of Cape Cod Light. Five officers and forty five men were on board. 0530 rigged ship for diving, except for bow planes, main induction, and conning tower hatch. Recognition and emergency identification information was kept written in chalk on the inside of bridge inclosure. Two lookouts, one quartermaster, and the Officer-of-the-Deck composed the bridge watch. 0726 entered Area FOUR and immediately dived to avoid detection by a navy supply ship (unidentified). 0800 sighted DD/SS Target Group. 0915 sighted two U.S. Destroyers on course 080, went to battle stations submerged and started approach. Discovered that Destroyers were not flying BAKER so abandoned attack and went to 100 feet and found static trim. 1005 received message on JK from DD416 "Fire Smoke Bomb". Fired black smoke bomb at 1009. 1016 surfaced and received visual signal from USS WALKE "DD416" directing this vessel to rendezvous with USS O'BRIEN and USS WALKE (Reference CSS-5 181310). Commenced conducting COMDESLANT Sound Exercises One A and Two A. 1203 completed exercises with USS O'BRIEN and USS WALKE. These vessels reported poor sound results. 1220 dived to avoid detection by blimp. Went to 75 feet and found static trim. 1346 surfaced. 1400 dived again to avoid blimp. 1500 surfaced and started charging air and batteries. At 1833 sighted battleship (believed USS NEW YORK) on the horizon. 1835 dived and started approach. 1900 gave up approach as hopeless due to distance to track of six miles. 1939 sunset. Surfaced, started charge, running on one engine. Saw many small lights during night, but no darkened target. Three lookouts, one quartermaster, and the Officer-of-the-Deck composed the bridge watch at night.

At 0600, Tuesday morning, dived and found static trim at 80 feet. 0834 surfaced to rendezvous with USS O'BRIEN and USS WALKE (Reference CSS-5 182400). 0900 made contact and at 0910 dived. 1026 surfaced. 1039 dived. 1142 surfaced. At 1200 was on surface investigating cause of failure of green smoke float, and jamming of yellow smoke bomb, therefore sent noon position with flat top antenna instead of periscope antenna 1205 dived and went to deep depth due to rain and reduced visibility. Found stop trim could be obtained at any depth between 60 and 110 feet. Within these depths large numbers of minute sea life could be seen through conning tower eye ports. Believe these were responsible for poor sound results during last two days. It is also believed that they may cause or may indicate the water layers which permit a stop trim. 1753 surfaced. It is inter-

-1-

SS136/A4-3
Serial 0192

U. S. S. S-31
SUBMARINE DIVISION FIFTY-TWO

August 23, 1941

CONFIDENTIAL

Subject: War Diary - War Patrol 18 August 1941 - 23 August 1941.

esting to note that during this last dive, evening meal was served while in static trim. Personnel both came aft to the after battery for dinner and came aft from the forward battery to permit watering of the battery. With all this change in weight, no difficulty was experienced in maintaining trim. There were no occurrences of interest during the night except experienced a short period of fog.

At 0555 on Wednesday, the Commanding Officer simulated a plane attack and sounded the diving alarm from the control room. Lookouts got below in good time. Submerged in one minute. Attempted to obtain static trim at periscope depth but was unsuccessful. Was able to obtain half switch trim in spite of moderate swells. 0800 attempted static trim at various depths down to 130 feet. Found this possible only between 60 and 70 feet. Again small sea life was found to exist at these depths permitting stop trim to the exclusion of other depths. 1146 heard what was believed might be a target. Came to periscope depth but found ship was a trawler. Again attempted static trim at periscope depth. Best attempt was for a period of eleven minutes. 1330 sighted a trawler headed directly toward us. Went to static trim at 80 feet. 1417 surfaced and at 1500 made contact with USS SEMMES in accordance with CSS-5 200125. Commenced exercises with USS SEMMES on surface, at periscope depth, and at 120 feet. At 0034 exercises with USS SEMMES completed. Commenced night patrol. No target sighted during the night.

At 0600, Thursday, August 21st., made quick dive to 125 feet; loaded two torpedoes, fired two water slugs at 100 feet; went to 150 feet, and then to 180 feet, using high speed and evasive tactics as for depth charge attack. Released lubricating oil through officers' head. Found temporary stop trim at 90 feet. Pulled two torpedoes from tubes under this trim. At 0704 made battle surface, using engines, and passing up shell tank through ammunition scuttle. Fired machine gun. 0811 dived and attempted to gain static trim and was unsuccessful at any depth. At 1000 surfaced to rendezvous with USS SEMMES. At 1100 instructions from CSS-5 directed this vessel to resume submerged patrol but as exercise with USS SEMMES was not completed, remained on surface until 1136. Shortly after diving, USS SEMMES passed within torpedo range, flying BAKER. Made torpedo approach, fired four water slugs and black smoke bomb. Surfaced at 1750. This vessel's attempt to get off noon position through periscope antenna was unsuccessful. Night patrol was uneventful.

-2-

SS136/A4-3
Serial 0192

U. S. S. S-31
SUBMARINE DIVISION FIFTY-TWO

August 23, 1941

CONFIDENTIAL

Subject: War Diary - War Patrol 18 August 1941 - 23 August 1941.

Friday, August 22nd., proved to be the most interesting day of the week. At 0820 sighted blimp and made a 35 second dive. At 0856 sighted ANTAEUS at a distance of 10,000 yards on course 160°T., presenting an angle on the bow of 80 degrees port. Attack was considered impossible but decided to take position for attack upon return of ANTAEUS. Best position for this was determined to be northwest corner of Area TWO. At 0920 sighted three Destroyers. Immediately commenced approach on Destroyers. During this approach at 1009 sighted two planes, believed to be biplane observation type headed to south eastward, flying in formation. At 1029 with leading Destroyer flying BAKER, made attack, firing four water slugs with straight bow settings. Did not fire smoke bomb as it was considered possible these vessels were conducting anti-aircraft practice and that smoke bomb would cause undue concern. The set up was unusually good as the three Destroyers at time of firing were apparently lying to and forming from this vessel a "C" such that if torpedoes missed the center ship they would certainly hit one on either side. Range at firing was 2000 yards. Upon completion this attack went at high speed to take position to intercept ANTAEUS on her return. 1115 again sighted blimp to eastward. 1149 sighted ANTAEUS hull down to eastward. At this time determined that ANTAEUS course would be too far north to permit attack while in Area TWO unless ANTAEUS were closed to eastward. But by so doing it would be possible to decrease the distance to the track only by high speed. Ran at 2500 amps a side. Finally, on northern limit of Option SIXTEEN at 12^h- 15^m- 18^{sec} LZT fired at estimated range of 700 yards, and estimated course of 271° T., as follows: #1 torpedo 15°right 55°track; #2 torpedo 10°right 60° track; #3 torpedo 5°right 65°track; #3 torpedo zero 70°track. Estimated speed 15 knots. On firing black smoke rocket was ordered fired but outer door jammed. Fired this rocket 3 minutes and 40 seconds after first tube was fired. After firing turned to course 090° T., and went to 80 feet at high speed, using evasive tactics. 1311 surfaced. 1728 Officer-of-the-Deck dived the boat to avoid detection by Destroyers. These Destroyers turned out to be contours of land. 1745 surfaced. 1839 Officer-of-the-Deck again dived to avoid what appeared to be two Destroyers in column formation presenting a 10° starboard angle on the bow. Went to normal approach course at high speed. Was just able to maintain steady bearing. After 30 minutes of running, discovered "Destroyers" were two sails on a lateen rigged sailing vessel on generally similar course. 1911 surfaced. Patrol during night was uneventful.

On Saturday, August 23rd., dived at 0612 to avoid sighting by merchant ship. 0809 surfaced. Arrived at anchorage at 1250. War Patrol completed.

-3-

SS136/A4-3 U. S. S. S-31
Serial 0192 SUBMARINE DIVISION FIFTY-TWO August 23, 1941

CONFIDENTIAL

Subject: War Diary - War Patrol 18 August 1941 - 23 August 1941.
General Remarks on Recommendations

1. This vessel is fitted with the Navy Yard, Philadelphia searchlight bracket. This has proved a vast improvement over the old mount. This same mount is also believed to offer the best machine gun mount yet devised for an S-class submarine. However, if a submarine were forced to remain on the surface, both machine gun and searchlight would be necessary. Thus, separate mounts should be provided.

2. The use of the searchlight shield has proved to be unsatisfactory under most circumstances. At 4000 yards, the USS SEMMES was challenged. She could not read this vessel's signals nor could this ship read hers. As recommended by the British, a brilliant light should be used for challenges.

3. The present periscope antenna which consists merely of an insulated cable suspended by a swivel on the top of number two periscope is believed of no value. Twice the cable fouled and pulled off of its securing on the top of the periscope. Also, changes of depth and wave action so change the effective antenna length that reception and transmission become wholly unreliable except under unusual conditions.

4. On this vessel's first dive, leaks along the binding bar between #2 main ballast tank and the forward battery room were discovered. On Monday night, seams along the binding bar were cold calked and the larger leaks were stopped. Due to the inaccessibility of the remaining seeps it was not found practicable to stop them. Because of this trouble, #2 main ballast tank was normally carried full with vent and kingston closed. It was found that this gave a desirable war time trim as the moment of #2 is just enough forward that on diving the bow planes will quickly take control. One dive of 35 seconds was made with this trim.

5. A hydrogen detector pump was found to be so badly worn that repairs could not be effected.

6. A gasket in the exhaust line between the port engine and the boiler blew and was repaired during a dive.

7. The ventilating blower for the starboard main motor became inoperative due to sheening of the coupling bolts to the fan. The inaccessibility of this motor made repairs impracticable.

8. The operation of the Nelseco Clarkson boiler has been a matter of guess and try due to the lack of detailed operating

-4-

SS136/A4-3
Serial 0192

U. S. S. S-31
SUBMARINE DIVISION FIFTY-TWO

August 23, 1941

CONFIDENTIAL

Subject: War Diary - War Patrol 18 August 1941 - 23 August 1941.

General Remarks on Recommendations (continued)

instructions. While operation has been satisfactory, it was possible during patrol to increase capacity by better operating procedure, from 14 gallons to 22 gallons per hour.

9. The signal gun while in proper adjustment has so much lost motion that its operation is unreliable. Considerable trouble during the patrol was experienced.

10. C&R air compressors, reinstalled upon recommissioning, have been a source of trouble due to lack of available parts and lack of available time for a thorough overhaul. The port compressor has performed satisfactorily but the starboard compressor is unable to hold third stage pressure. A major overhaul of this compressor was started about two months ago. Upon falling in with BEAVER, remainder of repair work will be completed.

11. The need of a ship's service store was felt. While these vessels used to have such, they have been abolished due to complications in administration. It is recommended that this vessel be authorized to have a "sweet-meats mess" of a total stock value of no more than $10.00 and that no reports or inventories be required except as found necessary by the Commanding Officer.

12. Sun glasses provided [illegible] issue were found unsatisfactory. Such glasses should be shielded from light on their sides, and heavy dark glasses should be provided for looking towards the early or late sun.

13. The morale of the crew was excellent. Some played Ace-Duce, checkers, and card games but most men slept when off watch. Food was good but there remains room for improvement which will be attained with training of commissary officer, cooks, and improvement to galley range. Cost of daily ration was considerably over ration allowance of fifty five cents.

M.L. ABELE,
Lieut-Comdr., U.S. Navy,
Commanding.

-5-

U.S.S. S-31

WAR PATROL DATA

(CONFIDENTIAL)

	Mon-18th 1st Day	Tues-19th 2nd Day	Wed-20th 3rd Day	Thur-21st 4th Day	Fri-22nd 5th Day	Sat-23rd 6th Day
ELECTRICITY						
1: Kilowatts discharged-auxiliary load surface	296	301	288.4	290.7	309	335
2: Kilowatts discharged-submerged	852	584.3	852	527.7	666	194
3: Kilowatts charged daily	1561	1315	1207	2851.9	1653.4	None
TEMPERATURES & HUMIDITY						
1: Daily high temperature	82	83	82	82	84	78
2: Daily low temperature	78	79	79	76	77	72
3: Daily high and low relative humidity	92 - 84	91 - 85	92 - 84	88 - 78	80 - 79	72 - 78
DIVING - STOPPED TRIM						
1: Hours of daily continuous stopped trim	1	6.2	1.6	0	0	0
2: Daily report on whether stopped trim can be obtained. Depth of stop trim	Yes 75 Ft	Yes 70 Ft	Yes 75 Ft	Yes & No	No attempt	No attempt
AIR BANKS						
1: Daily expenditures (Pounds)	1350	1000 each	800 each	1400	800	200
2: Amount charged daily (Pounds)	1350	1000 each	1000 each	0	2000	200
3: Hours compressors used daily	4 Port	1½ Port	1-3/4 Port	0	3	1½
POTABLE WATER						
1: Daily expenditure (Gallons)	162	90	110	181	126	61
2: Daily water made	120	90	99	136	133	93
3: Average gallons made per hr. distillers in use	14	14	14.1	14.2	21.3	21.2
4: Expenditures per man (Gallons)	3.2	1.8	2.2	2.5	3.6	1.1
BATTERY WATER						
1: Expenditure from tank (Gallons)	0	25	0	0	0	0
2: Loss in battery (Gallons)	100	(..........250..........)				
3: Average daily expenditure total period (6 days)	(..........45.5 gallons daily average..........)					

-1-

U.S.S. S-31

(CONFIDENTIAL) WAR PATROL DATA

	Mon-18th 1st Day	Tues-19th 2nd Day	Wed-20th 3rd Day	Thur-21st 4th Day	Fri-22nd 5th Day	Sat-23rd 6th Day
1: Diving times (Seconds)	69	55	60	55	35	70
	110	65	70	50	47	
	59	58		52	70	
	57	55				
	63					
	40					
PROVISIONS						
1: Daily expenditures in pounds	291	334	350	360	360	290
2: Daily average cost of rations	0.5504	0.832	0.623	0.616	0.7566	0.6664
FUEL						
1: Amount used daily (Gallons)	396	356	369	608	582	219
2: Amount used propulsion (Gallons)	300	234	116	306	300	219
3: Amount used on charge	96	122	253	302	282	0

M.L. Abele

M.L. ABELE,
Lieut-Comdr., U.S.Navy,
Commanding USS S-31

-2-

S. and A. Form No. 333
October 1939

BILL OF FARE FOR THE GENERAL MESS

U.S.S. S-31

Week beginning August 18, 1941

	BREAKFAST	DINNER	SUPPER
MONDAY	Sliced oranges Cereals Fried bacon Hash brown potatoes French toast Coffee	Roast pork Mashed potatoes & gravy Buttered corn Apple sauce Cucumber salad Buttered carrots Baked apples Coffee	Stuffed peppers Potatoes au gratin Stewed tomatoes Combination salad Mixed fruits Jam Coffee
TUESDAY	Fresh fruit Cereals Creamed chipped beef Creamed potatoes Cinnamon toast Coffee	Boiled ham String beans-bacon Baked potato Fruit salad Canned fruit Iced tea	Roast beef Creamed potatoes Radishes Pears Bread pudding Coffee
WEDNESDAY	Fresh fruit Cereals Poached eggs Dry toast Coffee	Roast veal Baked potatoes(special) Asparagus salad Gravy Cherry pie Iced coffee	Boiled frankfurters Potato salad Cold baked beans Combination salad(chilled) Mixed fruits (canned) Coffee
THURSDAY	Fresh fruit Cereals Corned beef hash Hot corn bread Jam, Sirup Coffee	Assorted cold cuts Swiss cheese Baked macaroni, with cheese Shrimp salad Fruit jello Iced cocoa	Beef pot roast Creamed potatoes String beans Frozen fruit pudding Radishes Coffee
FRIDAY	Prunes Cereals Fried bacon Omelet with chipped bacon Toast Coffee	Creamed chicken Mashed potatoes, browned in oven. Creamed peas Toast Celery Apple pie Lemonade	Fried liver & bacon Fried potatoes Sliced tomatoes Rice pudding Jam Cocoa
SATURDAY	Figs Cereals Fried pork sausages Hot cakes & sirup Coffee	Fried steak & gravy Baked potatoes Buttered string beans Lettuce salad, cucumbers Biscuits Chocolate pudding Coffee	
SUNDAY			

Total estimated cost -- Total estimated rations -- Estimated ration cost per day $0.60

APPROVED: Respectfully submitted,

M.L. ABELE, H.D. SPRATLIN,

LtComdr., *U.S.N.*, *Commanding.* Ensign ~~Supply Corps~~, *U.S.N.*R *Supply Officer.*

16—11690

STATEMENT OF I[illegible]S TO GENERAL MESS AND [illegible] OF RATION DAILY

(When submitted as a Bill of [illegible], this side will also be used to show estimated quantities of ration components, costs, etc.)

U. S. S. .... , 19...

ARTICLES	Quantity	Unit price	Amount
BREAD			
Biscuit:			
Biscuit........lb.			
Crackers........lb.			
TOTAL........lb.			
Bread, fresh:			
Graham........lb.			
Rolls........lb.			
Rye........lb.			
Wheat........lb.			
TOTAL........lb.			
Flour:			
Buckwheat....lb.			
Corn meal....lb.			
Graham........lb.			
Wheat........lb.			
TOTAL........lb.			
MEATS			
Preserved:			
Bacon, canned lb.			
Beef, dried, sliced lb.			
Beef, corned, canned........lb.			
Codfish and haddock........lb.			
Headcheese....lb.			
Luncheon meat lb.			
Salmon........lb.			
Sardines........lb.			
Sausage, cervelat, and salami....lb.			
Sausage, Vienna lb.			
Tongue, beef, canned........lb.			
....			
TOTAL........lb.			
Salt or smoked:			
Bacon........lb.			
Beef, corned, bulk........lb.			
Ham, s.p........lb.			
Salt pork........lb.			
Sausage, bologna lb.			
Sausage, Braunschweiger....lb.			
Sausage, frankfurter........lb.			
Shoulder, s.p....lb.			
....			
TOTAL........lb.			
Fresh:			
Beef........lb.			
Beef hearts....lb.			
Beef liver........lb.			
Chicken........lb.			
Duck........lb.			
Fowl........lb.			
Fish........lb.			
Mutton........lb.			
Pork........lb.			
Sausage, liver, fresh........lb.			
Sausage, pork....lb.			
Veal........lb.			
Turkey........lb.			
TOTAL........lb.			
VEGETABLES			
Dried:			
Beans, kidney lb.			
Beans, lima....lb.			
Beans, navy....lb.			
TOTAL........lb.			
Canned:			
Asparagus........lb.			
Beans, string....lb.			
Beets........lb.			
Corn........lb.			
Peas........lb.			
Pumpkin........lb.			
Sauerkraut........lb.			
Spinach........lb.			
Tomatoes........lb.			
TOTAL........lb.			

ARTICLES	Quantity	Unit price	Amount
VEGETABLES—Continued			
Fresh:			
Asparagus........lb.			
Beans, lima....lb.			
Beans, string....lb.			
Beets........lb.			
Cabbage........lb.			
Carrots........lb.			
Cauliflower....lb.			
Celery........lb.			
Corn (cob)....lb.			
Cucumbers....lb.			
Eggplant........lb.			
Garlic........lb.			
Lettuce........lb.			
Okra........lb.			
Onions, dry....lb.			
Onions, green..lb.			
Parsley........lb.			
Parsnips........lb.			
Peas, green....lb.			
Peppers, green lb.			
Peppers, red....lb.			
Potatoes, Irish lb.			
Potatoes, sweet lb.			
Pumpkin........lb.			
Radishes........lb.			
Rhubarb........lb.			
Spinach........lb.			
Squash........lb.			
Tomatoes........lb.			
Turnips........lb.			
........................lb.			
........................lb.			
TOTAL........lb.			
FRUITS			
Dried:			
Citron........lb.			
Coconut........lb.			
Cranberries....lb.			
Currants........lb.			
Raisins........lb.			
TOTAL........lb.			
Canned:			
Apples........lb.			
Apricots........lb.			
Cherries, red, sour, (water pack) lb.			
Figs........lb.			
Peaches........lb.			
Pears........lb.			
Pineapples....lb.			
Prunes........lb.			
TOTAL........lb.			
Preserved:			
Apple sauce....lb.			
Jams........lb.			
Mincemeat....lb.			
TOTAL........lb.			
Fresh:			
Apples........lb.			
Bananas........lb.			
Berries........lb.			
Cantaloups....lb.			
Cherries........lb.			
Grapes........lb.			
Grapefruit....lb.			
Lemons........lb.			
Melons........lb.			
Oranges........lb.			
Peaches........lb.			
Pears........lb.			
Pineapple....lb.			

ARTICLES	Quantity	Unit price	Amount
FRUITS—Con.			
Fresh—Continued			
Plums........lb.			
Tangerines....lb.			
........................lb.			
........................lb.			
TOTAL........lb.			
BEVERAGES			
Cocoa........lb.			
Coffee........lb.			
Tea........lb.			
TOTAL........lb.			
MILK			
Dry, whole....lb.			
Evaporated....lb.			
Fresh........qt.			
....			
BUTTER			
Fresh........lb.			
CEREALS, RICE, ETC.			
Barley........lb.			
Cereals, ready-to-eat........lb.			
Cornstarch....lb.			
Hominy........lb.			
Macaroni........lb.			
Oats, rolled....lb.			
Rice........lb.			
Tapioca........lb.			
TOTAL........lb.			
CHEESE			
Fresh........lb.			
EGGS........doz.			
LARD AND SUBSTITUTES....lb.			
OILS, SAUCES, AND VINEGAR			
Catsup, tomato gal.			
Horseradish, prepared........gal.			
Oil, salad........gal.			
Sauce, Worc....gal.			
Vinegar........gal.			
TOTAL........gal.			
SUGAR			
Granulated....lb.			
Powdered........lb.			
TOTAL........lb.			
BAKING POWDER........lb.			
BAKING SODA lb.			
FLAVORING			
Lemon........gal.			
Orange........gal.			
Vanilla........gal.			
MUSTARD........lb.			
PEPPER, black lb.			
PEPPER, red....lb.			
PICKLES........lb.			
SALT........lb.			
SIRUP........gal.			
SPICES........lb.			
YEAST........lb.			
HOPS........lb.			
MISCELLANEOUS			
....			
....			
....			
....			
....			
....			
....			
....			

REFRIGERATOR TEMPERATURES

Compartment	6 a. m.	3 p. m.
Meats........		
Vegetables........		
Butter and eggs........		

Approved:

....

.... *Supply Corps, U. S. Navy.*

16—11500

Number daily rations........................

Cost of ration per day, $........................

Respectfully submitted:

....

Chief Commissary Steward, U. S. Navy

901

S-31 1st WP

U. S. S. S-30 Flagship
SUBMARINE DIVISION 52

FB52/A16

Serial 07

CONFIDENTIAL

Ns

% Postmaster, New York, N.Y.,
April 7, 1942.

From: The Commander Submarine Division Fifty-Two.
To : The Commander-in-Chief, U. S. Fleet.
The Commander-in-Chief, Atlantic Fleet.
The Commander Submarines, Atlantic Fleet.

Subject: Report of War Patrol.

Reference: (a) Comsublant ltr. 14-41, file A6-5 (1979) of December 15, 1941.
(b) Comsublant conf. ltr. No. 2CL-42 of February 27, 1942.

1. The S-30, S-31, S-32, and S-33 conducted their first War Patrol in the Panama Area from March 10 to March 31, 1942.

2. No enemy contacts were made.

3. Radio reception was fair to good. Submarine Fox schedules were copied with difficulty and with no success on loop antenna while submerged. Naval Radio Balboa could be heard down to fifty feet on the loop antenna.

4. Training was carried out by simulated surface and submerged attacks, firing of small arms and the deck gun, using service ammunition, and appropriate drills. Balancing tests were very successful and boats could be balanced indefinitely between 60 and 110 feet.

5. The S-32 stopped and investigated a large unarmed fishing vessel on March 13 in latitude 5° - 46'N, longitude 86° - 30'W. Investigation disclosed that she was the United States vessel S. S. ATLANTIC, Registry No. F-700, Master Leslie Swanson, Home port San Diego, Calif., Destination - Fishing Grounds.

CHAS. W. GRAY.

Copy to: CSS-3
CSOSPPSFF
S-30
S-31
S-32
S-33

U.S.S. S-31
c/o Fleet Post Office
San Francisco, California

SS136/A16-3

Serial: 137

27 November 1944.

CONFIDENTIAL

From: The Commanding Officer.
To : The Commander Submarine Squadron FORTY-FIVE.

Subject: U.S.S. S-31 First and Second Patrols - Information on.

Reference: (a) ComSubRon 45 Conf. Ltr. FC5-45/A16-3, Ser. 0217 of 8 November 1944.

1. In compliance with reference (a) the following information is submitted:

(a) This command has none of the missing patrol reports concerned in file.
(b) The inclusive dates of the First Patrol are: 10 March to 31 March 1942. FILMED 97812
The inclusive dates of the Second Patrol are: 14 April to 13 May 1942.
(c) The Immediate Superior in Command at the time the patrols were made was: FILMED 116631
Commander Submarine Division FIFTY-TWO.
(d) The Commanding Officer:
Lieutenant Thomas F. Williamson, U.S. Navy.

W. N. DURLEY.

2 02213

Enclosure (E) 9

FB52/A16

U.S.S. S-30, Flagship
SUBMARINE DIVISION 52

Ns

Serial 020

% Postmaster, New York, NY,
May 15, 1942

C O N F I D E N T I A L

From: The Commander Submarine Division FIFTY-TWO.
To : The Commander Submarines, Atlantic Fleet.
Via : The Commander Submarine Squadron THREE.

Subject: Submarine Division Fifty-Two - Operations during period April 14 to May 13, 1942.

Reference: (a) Submarines Atlantic Fleet Conf. Ltr. 20L-42.
(b) Atlantic Fleet Conf. ltr. 7CL-42.

1. Submarine Division Fifty-Two was maintained as a Striking Force during the subject period consequently this report is submitted in lieu of that required by reference (a). Cocos Island was used as a base by the S-31 and S-32 from April 13 to April 24 and by the S-30 and S-33 from April 24 to May 2, 1942. The Gulf of Dulce was used as a base by the entire unit during the remainder of the period.

2. There were no enemy contacts.

3. No material defects were experienced which would prevent continued operation on mission.

4. The health of the crew was excellent and the habitability of the boats satisfactory.

5. Miles steamed surface and submerged by the individual boats:-

BOAT	SURFACE	SUBMERGED
S-30	2240 (engines)	58
S-31	2134 (engines)	84
S-32	2315 (engines)	60
S-33	2347 (engines)	50

6. Fuel oil expended:-

S-30 - 13,330 gallons.
S-31 - 14,682 gallons.
S-32 - 14,085 gallons.
S-33 - 14,400 gallons.

-1-

Enclosure (B) 5

FB52/A16

U.S.S. S-30, Flagship
SUBMARINE DIVISION 52

Ns

Serial 020

% Postmaster, New York, NY,
May 15, 1942.

C O N F I D E N T I A L

Subject: Submarine Division Fifty-Two - Operations during period April 14 to May 13, 1942.

- -

7. Factors of Endurance Remaining:-

BOAT	TORPEDOES	FUEL	PROVISIONS(DAYS)	FRESH WATER	PERS.DAYS
S-30	12	15780 gal.	10	410 gals.	14
S-31	12	14,723 gal.	10	650 gals.	10
S-32	12	14,074 gal.	10	645 gals.	14
S-33	12	14,000 gal.	10	850 gals.	10

8. The period at the Gulf of Dulce was utilized for training using the ANTAEUS as a target for day operations and a submarine for night operations. Daylight approaches were made by all officers having sufficient experience. Day Surprise and Night Surprise Attacks were made by all watch officers. Reserve Crews were trained daily on their own boats. Officers ready for qualification were qualified. Torpedo reloads were made by all boats. Pointer groups were trained and crews instructed in use of small arms. Each submarine fired D.T.P Prep. One torpedo was selected by lot from those maintained in the tubes for the past three months. All torpedoes ran normal except that of the S-31 which ran shallow striking the ANTAEUS and sinking. The intensive period of training contributed immensely in advancing the effeciency of this unit for continued war operations.

9. Attention is invited to the ideal location and the suitability of the Gulf of Dulce for short periods of training for new construction enroute to new stations.

CHAS. W. GRAY.

6

1st Copy

TG8.5/A16-3
Serial (07)

August 11, 1942.

DECLASSIFIED.

From: Commander Task Group Eight Point Five.
To : The Commander Submarines, Pacific Fleet.

Subject: War Patrol - U.S.S. S-31, report of. #3

Enclosure: (A) Report of Third War Patrol, U.S.S. S-31.
(B) Comsubron Forty-Five Confid. ltr., File FC45/A16-3 Serial (02) dated August 11, 1942.

1. This patrol extended for a period of thirty-six days. Twenty-nine days were spent on various stations in the Aleutian area. The only enemy contacts were with planes. The two instances in which use was made of plain language despatches to report enemy planes were justified by the tactical situation, but the procedure laid down in Paragraph 1178 PAC-70 was not followed.

2. During the bombardment of Kiska on August 7 the S-31 maintained position in the western reaches of Rat Island Pass, thereby preventing undetected departure of enemy ships from Kiska Harbor in the direction of retirement of the main Body. Better than average visibility made this position in confined waters relatively safe, without the aid of a fathometer, in spite of erratic currents.

3. The zone description of times set forth in this report is not given. It appears, however, that times are "XRAY".

4. The Commanding Officer received a serious chest injury from the explosion of a Mark X Emergency Identification Flare on August 10, when off Bogoslof Island, about sixty miles from Dutch Harbor. Use of these flares was ordered discontinued on July 13, 1942. Conditions permitted removal of the Commanding Officer to the Naval Air Station, Dutch Harbor in a PBY. In this connection, the recommendation that a pharmacist's mate be added to the complement of SAIL class submarines is strongly endorsed.

-1-

ENCLOSURE "B"

FC45/A16-3
Serial (02) August 11, 1942.

CONFIDENTIAL

From: The Commander Submarine Squadron FORTY-FIVE.
To : The Commander Submarines, PACIFIC FLEET.

Subject: U.S.S. S-31 - Third Patrol Report.

1. The material condition of the S-31 was excellent. The casualties which occurred did not interfere with the completion of the patrol. A recurrence of the casualty caused by the failure of the torpedo tube solenoid valve will be prevented by maintaining air on the individual tube solenoid valves instead of on the master solenoid valves.

2. All SAIL class submarines operating in this area have experienced trouble with loose superstructure plates. It is recommended that a project incorporating the principles of the alterations suggested by the Commanding Officer of the S-31 be undertaken by the Bureau of Ships with a view towards accomplishment during the next navy yard overhaul of the submarines of this squadron.

3. It is recommended that the fathometers and radars be installed in the submarines of this squadron at the first opportunity. This equipment is essential for the efficient operation of submarines in this area.

4. The recommendation that a pharmacist's mate be included in the allowance of S-class submarines is concurred in.

Copy to: S-31

-1-

ENCLOSURE "B"

SS136/A9
Serial (02)

Subject: U.S.S. S-31 - Report of Third War Patrol. Period from 7 July 1942 to 10 August 1942.

- -

All time Plus Ten.

1. NARATIVE

7 July — Underway singly on patrol mission in accordance with ComTaskGroup 8.5 operation order 4-42. Mission - to patrol Area North of Aleutian Island chain between West longitudes 176 and 179, destroy enemy shipping and to report all enemy contacts. Primary mission offensive.

Two convoys in sight on clearing Dutch Harbor. One or more patroling aircraft constantly in sight during A.M. Weather clear, calm. Visibility 8 miles.

8 July — Enroute on surface. 2300 entered area.

9 July — Submarged patrol at periscope depth, closing Islands as visibility permitted and attempting to identify peaks. Photographed peaks through periscope. Duration of dive 17 hours - still daylight when surfaced.

10 July — Submerged patrol, periscope depth during A.M. P.M. - Entered Kuluk Bay, Adak Island on surface. Made through search of all anchorages between Adak Island and Great Sitkin Island with fllowing exceptions:- Laska Cove, Cabin Cove. Negative results. 1300 Sighted PBY distant 6 miles on westerly course. Plane sighted us when about 3 miles off. Exchanged recognition signals. 1730 Sighted same plane or similar one on easterly course through periscope.

11 July — Periscope patrol from 0430 to 2200. 0135 O.O.D. sighted floating mass, mistook for a ship, flooded tubes, got ready for attack. Later identified as mass of kelp. Suffered casualty to torpedo tube noted in paragraph 9.

12 July — Submerged and surface patrol. Suffered casualty to bow planes noted in paragraph 9.

13 July — Rough sea, low visibility. Sound watch at 75 feet. Impossible to remain at periscope depth at economical speed.

14 July — Very rough sea. Good visibility during P.M. Deep submergence and surface patrol.

15 July — Rough sea, low visibility. 75 feet and periscope patrol.

16 July — Low visibility. Periscope patrol.

-1- ENCLOSURE "B"

CONFIDENTIAL
Subject: U.S.S. S-31 – Report of Third War Patrol

17 July — Low visibility forenoon. Good visibility from 1100 – 1230. At 1130, on surface, sighted 3 Army 4 motor bombers on course 270°, distant 5 miles. Bombers sighted us when about 3 miles off and changed course to avoid. No recognition signals exchanged. Periscope patrol during periods of low visibility.

18 July — Visibility unlimited. Saw all the Islands in this area for the first time. Manuevered on surface to check charted positions of islands and photograph. See remarks under "navigation".
Attempted to enter Bay of Islands, Adak Island, but place was full of fog.
1210 sighted PBY about 8 miles to the East. We apparently were not sighted.

19 July — Received orders from ComTaskGroup 8.5 to take new position bearing 325 distant 85 miles from Sirius Point, Kiska Island, being in position by day light, 22 July, Dutch Harbor date. Ordered not to approach closer than 25 miles to Sirius Point except during an attack. Acknowledged dispatch.
Periscope and surface patrol during the day.

20 July — Periscope patrol during A.M. About noon visibility lifted and we spent the afternoon trying to get into the Bay of Islands and plotting peaks. Bay of Islands fog bound. This place seems to remain full of fog after the rest of the area clears.

21 July — Enroute new area on surface. Taking course North of assigned intervening areas as am not certain that everyone has the word we are coming through.

22 July — 0130 Arrived on station. Started patrolling line on surface. Received word that our forces (Task Force 8) expect to bombard Kiska at 1900 tonight. Our orders are to remain on the surface when practicable.
1900 Lying to flooded down with decks awash, going ahead to permit manuevering when visibility closes.

23 July — Sea making up from West. Visibility varying from 500 yards to 5 miles. Surface patrol.
1300 Received orders permitting submerged patrol.
P.M., – periscope patrol.

-2- ENCLOSURE "B"

CONFIDENTIAL

Subject: U.S.S. S-31 - Report of Third War Patrol

- -

24 July Received word from ComTaskGroup 8.5 that the attack on Kiska had not been made. Ordered to resume status off 22 July - this calls for surface patrol when practicable.

25 July Received word from ComTaskGroup 8.5 that attack on Kiska would be made on 27 July (Dutch Harbor date) or the first date thereafter weather permitted. Ordered to resume normal patrol status 25-26 July; on surface when practicable 27 July. For normal patrol procedure this vessel, see "remarks".

26 July Visibility low. Periscope patrol.

27 July Surface patrol in anticipation of attack scheduled for 1900 tonight. Visibility varying from low to fair. Sea calm. Wind S.W. 5 knots. Overcast. P.M. Received word attack might be made later than 1900. 2055 Received word that attack will be made at 2100. Visibility here 300 yards. 2200 Received word Jap Auxiliaries and destroyer leaving Kiska course north. Took station vicinity 177 E, - 52-45 N in attempt to intercept them in case they head for Attu. Visibilty 200 yards.

28 July Visibility very low. Headed north at slow speed in hope of visibility and a shot at last nights convoy. 1300 Received word from ComTaskGroup 8.5 that attack apparently did not come off. Ordered to resume normal patrol procedure.

29 July Visibility varying. Periscope and surface patrol.

30 July Visibility good. Surface patrol.
1400 Received word TRITON returning to base due to breakdown. Ordered to take patrol position 25 miles S.W. of present position. Altered course accordingly.
1530 Received word attack on Kiska by main body deferred.
1730 Received orders from ComTaskGroup 8.5 shifting positions of all submarines and calling some back to base. We are ordered to area designated by "RATAM", East of Kiska and included between, Little Sitkin, Rat, Amchitka, Semisopochnoi Islands and including Amchitka Pass. Will leave present area tonight at 2000.

-3- ENCLOSURE "B"

CONFIDENTIAL

Subject: U.S.S. S-31 - Report ofThird War Patrol.

- -

31 July Enroute new area.
1118 While cruising at periscope depth while awaiting visibility to get fix before attempting to pass through islands, sighted submarine on surface identified as S-type - probably S-28.
Closed to 500 yards on his quarter to definitly identify before firing our recognition signal and surfacing, when he sighted our periscope and dove. We went to 125 feet in case he should fire.
2000 Entered area.

1 Aug. Visibility very low. Position in area unknown. Remained on surface during day trying to get fix. Received word another attempt by main body will be made on Kiska about 7 August.
1500 Obtained doubtful fix off Constantine Harbor. This area required caution as it is surrounded by islands and has very little sea room. Currents unknown.

2 Aug. Spent morning lying to with about 200 yards visibility. Position unknown.
Visibility good during P.M. Started checking anchorages in area on surface.

3 Aug. A.M. visibility good. Periscope patrol between Little Sitkin and Rat Islands.
1310 Surfaced. Sighted Jap 4 motor flying boat over Litte Sitkin. Dove. Patrol plane did not sight us. Circled area and returned to Kiska. Continued periscope patrol.

4 Aug. Visibility excellent. Searched (on surface) following anchorages; Constantine Harbor, Kirilof Bay, Northeast Coast Amchitka Island, North Coast Rat Island, including Gunner's Cove. Negative results.
2215 Sighted patrol plane off Little Sitkin Island. Darkness and distance prevented identification. As these planes have been bombing our advance base at Atka and his course was east, made plain language contact report.

5 Aug. Periscope patrol between Rat and Little Sitkin Islands. Visibility excellent.
Received modification to area Batam extending it to line between Sea Lion Rock and Segula Island - about 15 miles from Kiska Harbor.
In afternoon sighted, through periscope two bi-planes, seaplanes - assumed Japs out of Kiska. Disappeared into a cloud bank.

-4- ENCLOSURE "B"

CONFIDENTIAL

Subject: U.S.S. S-31 - Report of Third War Patrol.

---

6 August — Periscope patrol South of Segula Island. Visibility excellent. Entire West Coast of Kiska Island visible excepting harbor. No shipping sighted. 0707 While proceedingto entrance Rat Island Pass on surface, sighted PBY approaching from N.E. Dove to avoid him. 0928 Sighted small plane through periscope passing into cloud before details could be made out. 1435 Heard 15 distant underwater explosions in North Westerly direction. Sounded like bombs or depth charges. Visibility reduced to 1 mile about 1900. Surfaced and cleared Pass because of navigational restrictions.

7 August — This is day scheduled for attack on Kisk by our task force main body. Visibility low until 0900 at which time entered Rat Island Pass. Started periscope patrol in Rat Island Pass at western limit our area. Visibilit good. Kiska visible. 1530 Sighted Jap four motor twin tail flying boat on easterly course. After he had passed over, surfaced to send contact report. On surfacing sighted same plane or another just like it circling about four miles to south west. Able to broadcast contact three times in plain English on 450 KC before he sighted us and forced us under. Jap flyir boats observed periodically over Rat Island Pass and East Coast of Kiska for rest of afternoon. 1825 Surfaced to see if there was any sign of action by our forces. Kiska visible - nothing unusual heard or sighted. Dove. 1912 Sighted 4 PBY's over Kiska. 2117 Surfaced. 2147 Forced under by Jap flying boat. 2230(dark) surfaced and cleared Pass. Visibility 1000 yards. After surfacing received word that bombardmnt by our forces had been completed and ordered to return to Dutch Harbor leaving area after dark on the 8th.

8 August — Visibility in area very low. Unable to enter Rat Island Pass.

9 August — 0130 Left area. Enroute Base.

10 August — Enroute Base. Arrived Dutch Harbor.

 ENCLOSURE "B"

CONFIDENTIAL

Subject: U.S.S. S-31 - Report of Third War Patrol.

- -

2. WEATHER

The usual weather encountered was moderate sea, 10 knot wind from southwest, sky obscured by low lying clouds or fog, and limited visibility. The visibility was less than 2 miles for about 85% of the time.

Visibility varied rapidly and radically, often changing from 200 yards to 5 miles, or vice versa, in a period of a few minutes. Often the fog seemed to rise 200 or 300 feet above the surface of the ocean, to hang there for a while then suddenly drop. The fog was very wet, often becoming a drizzling rain with no definite point of transition. A hard rain was rare.

The wind was consistently from the southwest and usually about 10 knots. On two occasions it increased to storm force, still from the southwest, and held this force for about 36 hours before slacking off. The sea followed the wind exactly - usually moderate from southwest, increasing to very rough for two periods of about 36 hours each.

The temperature remained close to 50° during the patrol period

3. Tidal Information .

Currents encountered were variable and unpredictable, though not, as a rule, strong. Except in the "Ratam" area, no data was obtained close to the Islands, but off shore, no currents of over 0.8 knots were found. They usually ran less than 0.5 knots.

Currents found off shore in Adak North were in all quadrants, but about half were setting between North and East and about one quarter between South and West. Currents setting between north and east had an average drift of 0.4 knots with a maximum of 0.8 knots, and those with a southeasterly set averaged 0.3 knots with a maximum of 0.5 knots. No relation could be found between the currents encountered andthe tide tables. Currents close to the islands in this area are believed to be strong.

Currents to the northwest of Kiska could not be calculated as accurately due to lackof landfalls, but they appeared to set fairly constantly to the northeast with a drift of 0.4 knots. This drift was increased by as much as 0.5 knots by a strong southwest wind.

Near the center of the Ratam area, between Amchitka and Semisopochnoi Islands, the average current over a period of 13 or 25 hours invariably set southeast with a drift of from 0.4

-6- ENCLOSURE "B"

CONFIDENTIAL

Subject: U.S.S. S-31 - Report of Third War Patrol

to 0.8 knots. However, there is a definete ebb and flood throughout the area, corresponding roughly to the rise and fall of the tides at Kiska Harbor. The flood sets about 325 T at 0.5 to 1.0 knots and the ebb setting 130 T at 0.5 to 2.0 knots. In Rat Island Pass the currents appear to be no stronger than in the larger area but set about 305 and 145 degrees true. Throughout the area the set becomes erratic at the times of slack water at Kiska.

4. NAVIGATIONAL AIDS

Navigation in this area is not, at best, up to the standard to which we have grown accustomed for comfort. Plotted positions of islands, when seen, are often in error and celestrial observations are rare, either due to overcast or no horizon. Soundings with a hand lead are of no value. During the patrol no star sights were obtained and sun sights averaged one questionable sight a day. Currents were unknown and suspected strong near the islands. The lack of a fathometer was keenly felt.

The navigator, Lieutenant H.D. Sipple, spent considerable effort plotting the islands bordering area "Adak North". While this work was secondary to our mission and performed under adverse conditions, it is believed that his work is fairly accurate, certainly more accurate than the hydrographic chart available. Because of the few celestrial fixes possible, this plot more accurately shows the relative positions of the islands with one another than their geographical positions. They were plotted with Adak and Great Sitkin as bases. A copy of this plot is attached hereto.

The islands bordering "Ratam" are correctly shown on confidential Hydro Chart #5640. The United States Coast Pilot, Alaska, Part II, 1938 reports on page 375 that a small island was reported between Little Sitkin and Rat Island. This island does not exist and the passage north of Rat Island is clear and easily navigated. No information was obtained on the reef reported between Rat Island and Kiska.

Landfalls at first were very uncertain since low lying clouds and fog banks usually obscured all but an isolated tangent or single peak. A number of photographs of the islands were taken from various positions to facilitate recognition. These will be developed and printed on return to Dutch Harbor. This vessel has no official photography outfit - a private camera being used for this purpose.

-7-

CONFIDENTIAL

Subject: U.S.S. S-31 - Report of Third War Patrol.

5. ENEMY SHIPS SIGHTED

None.

6. AIRCRAFT SIGHTED

Date	Type	Position	Course	Altitude	Plus 10 time
July 10	1 PBY	Off Great Sitkin	270	1000	1330
July 10	1 PBY	Off Great Sitkin	090	800	1735
July 17	3 B-17 or B-24	52-17 N, 177-53 W	270	800	1130
Aug 3	1 Kawanisi 97	Over LittleSitkin	Circeling	2500	1358
Aug 4	Unidentified Patrol type	Over Little Sitkin	090	2000	2220
August 5	2 wing seaplanes(2)	Circling Ratam	Various	1000	1932
Aug 6	1 PBY	South of Semisopochnoi	S.W.	1000	0811
Aug 6	Small unidentified	Rat Island Pass	S.W.	800	0958
Aug 7	1 Kawanisi 97	Rat Island Pass	090	500	1530
Aug 7	1 Kawanisi 97	Over Kiska	Various	1000	1615
Aug 7	1 Kawanisi 97	Rat Island Pass	Various	1000	1700
Aug 7	4 PBY's	Over Kiska	Various	1500	1912
Aug 7	1 Kawanisi 97	Rat Island Pass	Various	1000	2147

7. SUMMARY OF ATTACKS

NONE

8. ENEMY A/S MEASURES

None encountered except indifferent aircraft patrol Rat Island Pass. Lookout parties may be stationed on Rat and Little Sitkin Islands to spot submarines on surface. Long daylight hours makes some surface cruising desirable to conserve battery in case of attack.

-7- -8- ENCLOSURE "B"

CONFIDENTIAL

Subject: U.S.S. S-31 - Report of Third War Patrol.

- -

5. ENEMY SHIPS SIGHTED

None.

6. AIRCRAFT SIGHTED

Date	Type	Position	Course	Altitude	Plus 10 time
July 10	1 PBY	Off Great Sitkin	270	1000	1330
July 10	1 PBY	Off Great Sitkin	090	800	1735
July 17	3 B-17 or B-24	52-17 N, 177-53 W	270	800	1130
Aug 3	1 Kawanisi 97	Over LittleSitkin	Circling	2500	1358
Aug 4	Unidentified Patrol type	Over Little Sitkin	090	2000	2220
August 5	2 wing seaplanes(2)	Circling Ratam	Various	1000	1932
Aug 6	1 PBY	South of Semisopochnoi	S.W.	1000	0811
Aug 6	Small unidentified	Rat Island Pass	S.W.	800	0958
Aug 7	1 Kawanisi 97	Rat Island Pass	090	500	1530
Aug 7	1 Kawanisi 97	Over Kiska	Various	1000	1615
Aug 7	1 Kawanisi 97	Rat Island Pass	Various	1000	1700
Aug 7	4 PBY's	Over Kiska	Various	1500	1912
Aug 7	1 Kawanisi 97	Rat Island Pass	Various	1000	2147

7. SUMMARY OF ATTACKS

NONE

8. ENEMY A/S MEASURES

None encountered except indifferent aircraft patrol Rat Island Pass. Lookout parties may be stationed on Rat and Little Sitkin Islands to spot submarines on surface. Long daylight hours makes some surface cruising desirable to conserve battery in case of attack.

-7- -8-

ENCLOSURE "B"

CONFIDENTIAL

Subject: U.S.S. S-31 - Report of Third War Patrol.

9. MAJOR DEFECTS EXPERIENCED

1. Failure of Torpedo Tube Solenoid Valve.

This failure, while not in itself a major defect, brought to light an important omission in torpedo tube upkeep and is reported for information.

At 0145 on July 11, the word was passed "make ready the bow tubes". One torpedoman was on watch. The tubes were in condition 3 - impulse tanks charges, master solenoid valve closed, tubes dry, outer doors closed, shutters open and torpedoroom in control of forward trim blow. The torpedoman on watch first opened the forward trim blow to flood the tubes (the fastest way to flood them on this boat as shown by experiment). Next he opened the master solenoid valve wide and started opening the outer doors. About 10 seconds after opening the master solenoid valve, the torpedo in #1 tube was heard to start and smoke came out of the inboard vent. The outer door to this tube had not yet been opened.

Investigation revealed that sufficient air had been admitted through the solenoid valve to lift the stop bolt and allow the torpedo to move forward with the motion of the boat and trip the starting lever. Check showed that the solenoid valve was leaking more air than the vent on the stop bolt cylinder could handle. It was not believed that the firing valve operated as there was no drop in impulse pressure and no blast of air was heard escaping from the inboard vent.

The solenoid valve was disassembled and found to be in good condition. When reassembled, it did not leak. Apparently some foreign object had lodged between the seat and disk, causing it to leak.

The routine on the torpedo tubes has been modified to include cracking the master solenoid valve daily and checking stop bolt vents for leaks.

The governor link on the torpedo was cut and the torpedo in no way injured. It was thoroughly checked and put back in service.

2. Bow planes.

On attempting to dive on 12 July, found that bow planes would not rig out. Check showed that the planes were attempting to tilt at the same time they swung to the out position, causing them to jam on the slots and frames of their housing. Planes were sprung clear with chain falls and pinch bar and, after 2½ hours work, rigged out. Tested and found to operate properly in the out position, except indicater was about 5 degrees out. The limit switch was altered to prevent planes from being housed to the point

-9- ENCLOSURE "B"

CONFIDENTIAL

Subject: U.S.S. S-31 - Report of Third War Patrol.

---

where they jammed and operations resumed. Planes now project about 3½ feet from the side of the ship when housed.

Cause of failure unknown. It will be investigated on return to base.

3. Leaks into reserve L.O. Tank and After Battery Tank.

Salt water was discovered in #8 fuel oil tank (in use as a reserve lub oil tank) and a mixture of salt water and fuel oil in the after battery well. From past experience this probably means a leak in the bulkhead betwwen #7 and#8 fuel oil tanks and leaks from #9 fuel oil tank and #3 main ballast tank along the bulkhead between the two into the after battery well. This condition has been corrected twice since recommissioning and seems to be due to structual vibrations around the engines. It is not believed that the condition is serious enough to warrant concern at the present. About 15 gallons of salt water were taken from #8 and about 15 gallons every ten days from the after battery well. Deepest depth reached during the patrol was 175 feet.

10. RADIO RECEPTION

Radio recebtion was good. Able to work N.P.M. on 8470 KC with signal strength varying from 3 to 5 in all areas. One contact report was delivered to Radio San Diego with strength 5 on this frequency. Dutch Harbor was received strength 4 on 8270 KC in area Adak North but we were unable to work them. However, it is believed that this fault lies with the Dutch receiving watch. As far as is known, received all messages originated in the Kiska area on 450 KC.

NPM fox was usually received without difficulty on 25.6 KC but on two occasions it was necessary to shift to 8230 KC to get them.

NPM fox on 25.6 KC could normally be copied at periscope depth using the loop antenna. NPM shifts to 30.6 KC from 2200 to 2300 Zed daily and could not be received submerged on this frequency.

11. SOUND

The only sound equipment installed is a topside J.K. Sound conditions seemed to be average or better than average - lack of targets precluded more accurate data.

One phenomena was noted which is still unexplained. In the Adak North and Ratan areas a beat similar to the sound of screws

-10- ENCLOSURE "B"

CONFIDENTIAL
Subject: U.S.S. S-31 - Report of Third War Patrol.

- -

but with a noticeable click superimposed was picked up three or four times a day. This beat had a definite frequency of about 75 a minute and at times would suddenly shift to double this frequency. Bearings by JK were definite and narrow. The bearing would usually remain in one sector, changing slowly, but at times would radically shift sixty or more degrees. The noise was usually very loud and best received on 18 kilocycles. At times two or more separate sources could be picked up. Changing course did not change the true bearing and changing speed and stopping the propellers was without effect. The noise came from some source other than this ship.

Careful plotting and visual searches revealed no clue to its identity except on two occasions whales were seen blowing on the reported bearing. Whales are numerous in these areas as are active volcanoes. Some explanation may be found in them. The noise was not heard northwest of Kiska, where fewer whales and no volcanos are found.

12. HEALTH AND HABITABILITY

The health of the crew was good except for common colds and an epidemic of sore throats. About ten days out the majority of officers and crew developed sore throats. It is guessed that this was caused by some bug transmitted through mess gear. Facilities do not permit proper disinfecting of mess gear. A number of colds developed but the number was surprisingly low considering the usual wet bridge and normal cold wet condition of the boat. Only one man was turned in with fever. A mess attendant developed a suspected venereal condition having the character s of chancroid. This man was discharged from the Naval Hospital in Philadelphia last December after treatment for this disease. It is suspected that this is a recurrence of the old case. Vitamin pills were used from the beginning of the patrol. Morale was excellent throughout. See "Remarks" concerning Pharmacist's Mate.

HABITABILITY

46 men and 5 officers were carried. Since only 38 crews bunks are installed "hot bunk" system of sleeping was necessary. Conditions seemed crowded at first, but crew soon became acclimated and made out very well. This isn't to say that an "S" boat in the Bering Sea is comfortable.

Three weeks fresh provisions were stretched over four weeks. Food for the fifth week all came out of cans.

- 11 - ENCLOSURE "B"

CONFIDENTIAL

Subject: U.S.S. S-31 - Report of Third War Patrol.

- -

13. MILES STEAMED

Miles to Adak North	421
Miles in Adak North	1116
Miles to N.W. Kiska	292
Miles in N.W. Kiska	1034
Miles to Ratam	131
Miles in Ratam	685
Miles to Dutch Harbor	470
Total miles steamed	4149

14. FUEL OIL EXPENDED

July 7 - 911 Gals.	July 19 - 507 Gals.	July 31 - 681 Gals.
8 - 1217 "	20 - 686 "	Aug. 1 - 375 "
9 - 437 "	21 - 1152 "	2 - 315 "
10 - 654 "	22 - 730 "	3 - 403 "
11 - 325 "	23 - 607 "	4 - 632 "
12 - 648 "	24 - 565 "	5 - 305 "
13 - 508 "	25 - 645 "	6 - 423 "
14 - 610 "	26 - 410 "	7 - 514 "
15 - 637 "	27 - 645 "	8 - 868 "
16 - 535 "	28- 750 "	9 - 1420 "
17 - 471 "	29- 480 "	10 - 1500 "
18 - 935 "	30- 554 "	11 - 870 "
		Total 23925

15. FACTORS OF ENDURANCE REMAINING

Torpedoes - Full allowance on board.
Fuel - About 4000 gallons remaining.
Provisions- 5 days canned, no fresh.
Fresh water- Tanks full
Personnel - Crew physically in good condition, However, notice growing tension and restless that would probably soon result in marked decrease in personnel efficiency.

16. FACTORS LIMITING ENDURANCE.

Endurance seems to be limited by all expendibles, (personnel, food, fuel and lub oil) to 35 - 40 days of slow cruising; similar to the one horse shay.

17. REMARKS

Patrol on surface when visibility extended beyond the horizon and chances of attack or sighting by planes smaller than flying boats slight. Flying boats are almost invariably picked up in time to dive before being sighted. Periscope depth patrol when visibility was limited and sea conditions permitted normal

- 12 - ENCLOSURE "B"

CONFIDENTIAL

Subject: U.S.S. S-31 - Report of Third War Patrol.

- -

parallel trim at periscope depth. 75 feet patrol with sound watch and half hour periscopeexposures when sea was rough. This necessitated by long hours of daylight (approximately 19) and the resultant necessary conservation of the battery for attacks.

Battery was floated during surface patrols. At night battery was charged withone engine, if not too low, and other engine out on screw. Otherwise we lay to and charged with both engines. This latter procedure was necessary about 35% of the time. Battery was charged by modified step-by-step method, 200 amp cuts being taken to cut down charging time. Battery was overcharged when practicable every 5 days. Battery was never gassed during daylight hours.

Normal routine was carried out by the crew, one of three sections on watch. If on surface, reveille was held at 1000 and 1600. Submerged all hands noton watch were allowed to sleep.

Superstructure.

Considerable trouble has been experienced with superstructure and side plating coming adrift. Usually the plating will rust through around the rivets atone corner, allowing the corner to flap. This not only interferes with sound reception, but makes the boat a perfect target for sound tracking.

Most of the plating on this ship was renewed during overhaul at Philadelphia last December. On a patrol in the Atlantic the following February, several of the new plates ripped loose. Hence it is believed that the material condition of the plates is not the trouble - the whole assembly is just not heavy enough to take the beating it gets in a rough sea.

Once the plating starts to go, it is most difficult to finish ripping the sections off withthe tools available. At the time of writing, we are off Kiska Island with two sections (just below the JK head) bent back at 90 degree angles and secured with 21 thread line in an attempt to cut down the noise. We are unable to cut the plates free. Such a condition has been usual on the three war patrols run thus far.

Because of this condition, it is recommended that the following alterations be authorized for early accomplishment:

1. Remove all superstructure, framing, side plating and decking except bow plane housing, gun sponson and section around conning tower fairwater.

- 1 3- ENCLOSURE "B"

CONFIDENTIAL

Subject: U.S.S. S-31 - Report ofThird War Patrol.

- -

2. Double the weight of the plating around the gun sponson and fair it into the pressure hull at its forward and after edges.

3. Cut off capstan shaft and lower capstan to pressure hull.

4. Remove "cigarette deck" and fairwater surrounding it.

5. Cut off capstan, submerged, anchor operating rods to lower to pressure hull.

6. Enclose submerged anchor cable drum in non-watertight housing (Note - deck anchor has already been removed).

7. Provide catwalk on pressure hull from gun sponson forward and conning tower aft. Provide center line life line.

8. Manufacture portable torpedo loading skids to be kept with spare torpedoes.

Since the only men allowed on deck during a war patrol are the bridge watch and gun's crew, the sections removed would not be missed. The surface silhouette of the ship would be reduced by about 50%. Present upkeep trouble with the superstructure would be eliminated. By breaking up the plane surface of the deck visibility from aircraft would possibly be reduced.

Pharmacist's Mate

It is highly recommended that the personnel allowance of this type of submarine be changed to include a pharmacist's mate. It is suggested that the yeoman might be left in port during patrols and the pharmacist's mate ride the boat in his place.

It is believed that the longer patrols of the Fleet type submarine allowing them a pharmacist's mate is more than offset by the poor habitability of this type; - in as much as constant dampness, "hot bunks", wet watch stander clothes and overcrowding all tend to lower the general health of the crew.

- 14 - ENCLOSURE "B"

1st copy

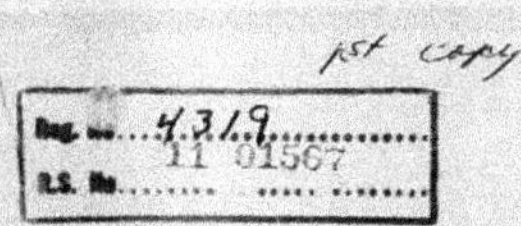

FF12-10/A16-3(5) SUBMARINE FORCE, PACIFIC FLEET Rs

Serial 01271

Care of Fleet Post Office,
San Francisco, California,
November 7, 1942.

DECLASSIFIED

COMSUBPAC PATROL REPORT NO 87
U.S.S. S-31 - FOURTH WAR PATROL.

From: The Commander Submarine Force, Pacific Fleet.
To : Submarine Force, Pacific Fleet.

Subject: U.S.S. S-31 - Report of Fourth War Patrol.

Enclosure: (A) ComTaskGroup 8.5 Conf ltr TG8.5/A16-3 Serial 032 of October 1, 1942.
(B) Comsubron 45 Conf ltr FC45/A16-3 Serial 037 of October 3, 1942.
(C) Copy of subject patrol report.

1. Subject report contains valuable information of existing weather conditions in the Aleutian area.

2. It appears that the greatest hazards encountered by the S-31 were the weather and our own planes. While nothing can be done about the former, the maximum exchange of all available operating information between submarines and aircraft command centers should be utilized to reduce the latter hazard to a minimum.

R. H. ENGLISH.

COMMANDER IN CHIEF
U.S. FLEET
RECEIVED
1942 NOV 24 12 12

DISTRIBUTION:
(35CM-42)
List III: SS
Special:
F1(5), EN3(5), Z1(5),
Comsublant (2)
Comsubsowespac (2).

E. R. SWINBURNE,
Flag Secretary.

43946 FILMED

TG8.5/A16-3
Serial 032

Naval Operating Base,
Dutch Harbor, Alaska,
October 1, 1942.

CONFIDENTIAL

From: The Commander Task Group Eight Point Five.
To : The Commander Submarines, Pacific Fleet.

Subject: U.S.S. S-31 - Report of Fourth War Patrol.

Enclosure: (A) Original and one copy of subject report.

1. All but four of the twenty-seven days on station during this patrol were spent in an area devoid of enemy activity. The thorough manner in which areas off KISKA were covered during the four days available is noted with approval. Over an extended period this energetic coverage should bring results.

2. In spite of the lack of enemy contacts this patrol was not uneventful, the S-31 being twice attacked by friendly planes, having chlorine gas in the forward battery on one occasion, and transferring at sea to a patrol plane a man suffering from a severe injury. One of the attacks by friendly planes, depth charges from a PBY, was due in part to the pilot not making sufficient allowance for errors in navigation in the proximity of an area in which attack restrictions had been established. The failure of the S-31, which had no emergency identification flares, to use as a smoke bomb for recognition signal is not understood. The other attack, surprise machine gunning by two P-39s, resulted from the pilots not being aware of the attack restrictions.

3. Attention is invited to the resume of weather submitted with the subject report.

4. The establishment of a DUTCH HARBOR submarine fox schedule is not considered necessary or desirable. The NPG FOX schedule is serving the purposes of the submarines in the North Pacific in a satisfactory manner. Efforts are continuing to improve the direct reception at DUTCH HARBOR of submarine transmissions.

ENCLOSURE (A)

FC45/A16-3
Serial 037

October 3, 1942.

CONFIDENTIAL

From: The Commander Submarine Squadron Forty-Five.
To : The Commander Submarines, Pacific Fleet.

Subject: U.S.S. S-31 - Fourth War Patrol.

1. The S-31 spent twenty-seven (27) days on station. Twenty-three (23) days were spent in an area covering an amphibious operation where enemy contacts were remote. No contacts were made with the enemy.

2. All major defects will be corrected during the refit period.

ENCLOSURE (B)

CONFIDENTIAL

Subject: U.S.S. S-31 - Report of Fourth War Patrol.

- -

Period from 26 August, 1942 to 28 September 1942.

1. NARRATIVE

26 August (Plus 10) Underway singly on patrol mission in accordance with ComTaskGroup 8.5 Operation Order 12-42. Mission to patrol assigned area, and to locate and destroy enemy surface forces approaching ADAK ISLAND. Weather overcast, seas rough from SW, visibility variable between 4 and 10 miles.

27 August (Plus 10) Enroute area on surface. Made trim dive. Sighted PBY and exchanged recognition signals. Sighted B-24, not detected. Visibility very poor, four miles maximum; seas and wind moderating, shifting from SW to W.

28 August (Plus 10) Enroute area on surface. Cleared AMUKTA PASS during night. Wind and sea choppy from N.E., weather clearing. 1257 Sighted unidentified plane on stbd bow distance 3 miles. Dived. Identified plane through periscope as PBY; he was attacking. Went to 125 feet, rigging for depth charge attack. 1301 Sharp explosion, probably bomb, astern distance about 300 yds. 1301½ Dull explosion, probably depth charge, on stbd quarter distance about 400 yds. 1303 c/c to 90° to left. 1305 Dull explosion, probably depth charge, astern distance 800 yds. 1535 Surfaced; proceeding to area, no damage done. 2200 Arrived in area.

29 August (Plus 10) Conducting submerged patrol; assume we must not be seen today in view of tomorrow's operations. Gave torpedoes routine check. Exercised crew at emergency drills. Experimented with backing down while submerged. Position is doubtful; have seen no sun or stars since departure Dutch. Visibility poor.

30 August (Plus 10) In view doubtful position, set course for ADAK in order try to make landfall. 1300 Visibility closed in so badly considered dangerous to maintain course in view suspected proximity of land; changed course to South. High seas and about a forty knot wind E, ceiling 200 feet with less than 2 miles visibility. So much water down conning tower hatch that we tried cruising with the conning tower hatch closed and main and auxiliary inductions open. Water entered through both inductions. Chlorine in forward battery compartment (see paragraph 9). 1605 Man injured due to heavy seas (see paragraph 12.).

31 August (Plus 10) Conducting periscope patrol. Obtained position from sight of moon and sun in A.M. Surface visibility fair.

-1- ENCLOSURE (C)

CONFIDENTIAL

Subject: U.S.S. S-31 - Report of Fourth War Patrol.

- -

1 Sept. (Plus 10) Conducting submerged patrol at 90 feet, planing up every half hour to 36 feet. Poor visibility. Experienced maximum 15° roll at 90 feet due to heavy seas. Watered batteries.

2 Sept. (Plus 10) Conducting surface patrol. Visibility unlimited; ceiling unlimited. Dived for unidentified plane. Routine check on torpedoes during dive. Received word GATO passing through area today.

3 Sept. (Plus 10) Conducting surface patrol. Visibility unlimited; ceiling unlimited. Dived for PBY - want to get O.O.D.'s in habit of diving for planes in enemy waters. Received word ---- will not be occupied; S-31 to stay in --- .

4 Sept. (Plus 10) Conducting surface patrol. Visibility fair. 1050 Dived; weather closed in; conducting periscope patrol. Barometer dropping.

5 Sept. (Plus 10) Conducting surface patrol. Visibility good. Barometer steady. Received word GATO to -- .

6 Sept. (Plus 10) Conducting surface patrol. Visibility good. 1000 Submerged to give torpedoes routine check; exercised crew at emergency drills and battle stations.

7 Sept. (Plus 10) Conducting surface patrol. Visibility good. 1143 Submerged after sighting unidentified plane approaching at high speed from the east. O.O.D. claimed plane was "ZERO" fighter; lookout claimed plane appeared to be larger. However, when plane sighted, it was very low over water, distance about four miles, and was heading directly towards us. C.O. took good sweep while submerging but saw no plane. In view of fact that plane could have been "ZERO" thus indicating enemy CV in vicinity, course was set to intercept any possible enemy forces approaching from west, and a periscope patrol was maintained during the remainder of the day.

8 Sept. (Plus 10) Conducting surface patrol; excellent visibility. At 1402 a man was seriously injured necessitating calling for a PBY to get him to a hospital. Arrangements were made and rendezvous was effected at 1900 at point 65. After transfer of man returned to area (see paragraph 12).

9 Sept. Conducting surface patrol, excellent visibility. Dived for PBY for half hour. Received word that new area ---- is to be formed, concelling -- and --.

-2- ENCLOSURE (C)

<u>CONFIDENTIAL</u>

Subject: U.S.S. S-31 - Report of Fourth War Patrol.

- -

10 Sept (Plus 10)	Received word to proceed to new area __, arriving before daylight. 0600 Arrived area. Conducting surface patrol. Heretofore have been diving for all planes, but this area is too prolific; sighted sixteen planes, mostly Army and began exchanging recognition signals upon close approach.
11 Sept (Plus 10)	Conducting surface patrol; excellent visibility. Sighted one PBY; exchanged recognition signals.
12 Sept (Plus 10)	Conducting surface patrol; excellent visibility. Sighted twelve planes during day, all friendly. Between 1905 and 1940 sighted fifteen puffs of smoke which appeared to be bomb explosions between bearings of 258°T and 272°T about twenty miles distance. All were in the area near AMATIGNAK ISLAND. Proceeded out of area to investigate. Could see nothing before darkness; sighted no aircraft. Two large pillars of smoke, which could have been damaged ship, disappeared to the west faster than we could close. No report made in view of fact that if any action took place our forces would make report.
13 Sept (Plus 10)	Conducting surface patrol; excellent visibility. Sighted two PBY's and exchanged recognition signals. At 1413, while 8 miles south of ADAK ISLAND and just west of KAGALASKA STRAIGHT, the O.O.D., lookout and quartermaster sighted two "ZERO" fighters low over water, distance five miles, headed for us at high speed. Dived, but not fast enough, since two short bursts of M.G. bullets were heard against the hull and in the water. Island background had camaflouged the planes until they were close aboard. Surfaced and sent coded contact to CTG 8.5 upon surfacing saw much air activity in vicinity of KULUK BAY. Several large planes followed closely by smaller planes were seen circling KULUK area, but identification could not be established at a distance of 20 miles. Retired to southern part of area.
14 Sept (Plus 10)	Received word from C.T.G. 8.5 that P-38's attacked us yesterday. O.O.D., lookout, and quartermaster retain original opinion. Conducting surface patrol in A.M., excellent visibility; submerged patrol P.M., weather closed in. Sighted three PBY's. Watered batteries; gave torpedoes routine check.
15 Sept (Plus 10)	Conducting surface and submerged patrol; visibility excellent in A.M., but poor in P.M. Sighted three PBY's.

ENCLOSURE (c)

-3-

CONFIDENTIAL

Subject: U.S.S. S-31 - Report of Fourth War Patrol.

- -

16 Sept (Plus 10) Good visibility; conducting surface patrol. Barometer dropping slowly.

17 Sept. (Plus 10) Conducting submerged patrol, visibility low during A.M., but increasing slightly in afternoon. Backed down for 1½ hours at normal parallel as an experiment.

18 Sept (Plus 10) Conducting surface patrol; excellent visibility; Dived twice for PBY's. Gave torpedoes routine check.

ENCLOSURE (C)

-4-

CONFIDENTIAL

Subject: U.S.S. S-31 - Report of Fourth War Patrol.

- -

19 Sept (Plus 10)	Conducting surface patrol; visibility excellent. Weather closing in at noon. Sighted PBY. Dived; conducting submerged patrol, periscope depth. Weather and visibility bad during P.M.
20 Sept (Plus 10)	Received word from C.T.G. 8.5 to proceed to new patrol area RATAN, leaving TIGER at darkness tonight. In view of all night run, decided to conduct surface patrol unless have to dive in order to save the battery. Visibility only fair. 2000 left area.
21 Sept (Plus 10)	Received word from C.T.G. 8.5 to leave RATAN area on morning of 23rd; DUTCH HARBOR time, and proceed to KISKA __ and __, leaving these areas for DUTCH at darkness the 24th, returning via southern route. 0600 entered area, conducting surface patrol. Observed CONSTANTINE BAY submerged from 2 - 3 miles; no signs of activity. 1535 unidentified plane, B-23(?), bombed CONSTANTINE HARBOR for half an hour; much smoke. Continued patrol to northward submerged. Surfaced in thick fog, 300 yds visibility. Hazardous navigation when foggy in RAT ISLANDS.
22 Sept (Plus 10)	Conducting surface patrol in thick weather. Desire to observe RAT ISLAND PASS and will not be able to get there if remain submerged in A.M. Having difficulty navigating due fog and unpredictable currents in such restricted area as RATAN. Forced to dive twice from one unidentified plane and one PBY. Gave torpedoes routine check during second dive. Made surface reconnaissance of RAT ISLAND PASS to western extremity. No enemy traffic. We go to KISKA __ and __ area tonite by way of OGLALA PASS. 2330 cleared OGLALA PASS.
23 Sept. (Plus 10)	Approaching VEGA BAY. Dived during darkness at 0639. Patrolling from VEGA POINT to ORIENT POINT at periscope depth maintaining patrol course along fifty fathom curve. Time submerged 14 hours and 22 minutes. Only signs of habitation were a few tents and a small shack on LITTLE KISKA ISLAND. Could not see into KISKA HARBOR. Weather excellent with few showers which cleared off rapidly. Retired to southwest during night to charge batteries and still cover any enemy traffic.
24 Sept (Plus 10)	Approaching VEGA BAY. Dived at daylight, conducting periscope patrol. Nothing in VEGA BAY that could be seen from 3 miles distance. Covering approaches to KISKA HARBOR from South. Observed KISKA HARBOR through SOUTH PASS; could see no ships; however view restricted to very small part of harbor to west of NORTH HEAD.

ENCLOSURE (C)

-5-

CONFIDENTIAL

Subject: U.S.S. S-31 - Report of Fourth War Patrol.

- -

	Leaving area; very surprising that we didn't see a single plane or surface ship for two days. Time submerged 14 hours and 02 minutes. Visibility and ceiling unlimited.
25 Sept (Plus 10)	Enroute DUTCH HARBOR. Cleared area KISKA at 0500. Dived once for PBY south of AMCHITKA PASS. Estimate can remain at sea another 10 days at slow speed.
26 Sept (Plus 10)	Enroute DUTCH HARBOR. Understand KISKA now full of ships; just missed them which is our bad luck.
27 Sept (Plus 10)	Enroute DUTCH HARBOR. 1200 passed 150 mile circle from DUTCH.
28 Sept (Plus 10)	Enroute DUTCH HARBOR. 0930 cleared AKUTAN PASS. 1332 moored Submarine Base, DUTCH HARBOR.

ENCLOSURE (C)

-6-

CONFIDENTIAL

Subject: U.S.S. S-31 - Report of Fourth WAR Patrol.

- -

2. Weather

For about 75% of the time the weather was the usual Aleutian type: Visibility, four to eight miles; sky overcast with a 300 - 500 foot ceiling; sea, rough and unpredictable as to direction; wind, following the sea with about a two point lag and varying from five to ten knots.

The fog only once became really dense, but it closed in at times with great speed and then dissipated just as fast. The fog sometimes developed into a light drizzle although a heavy rain was never encountered.

For five days, from September 9 - 13, the weather was unusually fair which is apparently a rare occurrence in these waters.

As a matter of aerological interest an itemized weather resume for the month of September in areas south of ADAK ISLAND, in the RAT ISLANDS, and south of KISKA ISLAND is attached.

When the weather is fair in this area it is possible to sight large planes such as PBY's and B-24's up to ranges of 25 miles very easily due to the exceptional clearness of the atmosphere.

The highest barometer reading recorded was 30.35" and the lowest was 29.16". It is not unusual for the barometer to vary as much as one inch in a 24 hour period.

During the two days spent in KISKA ___ and _____, the weather was unusually clear. In the mornings a fog shrouded the island but this cleared off by 1000 and during the rest of the day nearly all the RAT ISLAND group were in sight. Visibility in both afternoons was unlimited, the ceiling was unlimited, the sky had very few clouds, and during the night the moon was full and bright until about 0400 when a light fog and drizzle set in again.

ENCLOSURE (C)

-7-

CONFIDENTIAL

Subject: U.S.S. S-31 - Report of Fourth War Patrol.

- -

WEATHER RESUME

DATE	BAROMETER (AVERAGE)	TEMP (AVERAGE)	SEA	WIND Dir.	(FORCE)	Dir.	Vis. Mi.	SKY	CEILING
26	2985	58	Rough	SW	3	SW	4	OVC	200
27	3004	58	Swells	W	3	W	4	OVC	200'
28	3003	56	Choppy	NE	3	NE	U	High OVC	2000
29	2976	57	Choppy	E	2	E	U	High OVC	2000
30	2954	56	Turbulent	E	6	E	2	OVC	200'
31	2936	56	Heavy	ESE	2	ESE	10	High OVC	2000'
1	2945	56	Heavy	SW	3	SW	3-10	OVC	500'
2	3012	58	Swells	SW	1	SW	U	Clear	U
3	3029	59	Calm	W	0	-	U	Clear	U
4	3003	56	Heavy	SE	4	ESE	5-1	OVE	300'
5	2965	56	Heavy	SW	5	SSW	5-3	OVC	500'
6	2973	56	Heavy	SW	6	SSW	6-3	OVC	500'
7	2985	55	Swells	WSE	4	SW	5-8	OVC	1000'
8	2996	56	Choppy	WNW	2	WNW	8-10	OVC	1000'
9	3007	56	Swells	W	3	W	8-10	OVC	1500'
10	3004	56	Calm	W	0	-	U	OVC	2500'
11	[illegible]	56	Calm	E	0	-	U	U	30,000'
12	[illegible]	56	Calm	E	0	-	U	OVC	3500'
13	3021	56	Calm	SE	0	-	18-U	OVC ptly	3500'
14	3010	55	Choppy	ENE	2	E	5-15	OVC	2000'
15	2982	55	Swells	NE	2	NE	2-10	OVC	300'
16	2966	54	Rough	NW	4	NW	5-10	OVC	300'
17	[illegible]	55	Rough	SW	4	SW	2-10	OVC	200-2000
18	2943	55	Choppy	NE	4	NE	15-20	OVC	1500'
19	2927	54	Rough	NW	4	NW	2-20	OVC	1000'
20	2926	54	Rough	NW	4	NW	5-15	OVC	200'
21 *	2954	51 -	Swells	NW	4	NW	0-6	OVC	0-1000'
22	2952	51 -	Swells	NW	4	NW	0-6	OVC	0-300'
23	2942	50 -	Swells	NW	4	NW	3-10	OVC	3000'
24	2945	55	Swells	NW	3	NW	3-U	OVC-U	300'-U
25	2956	51	Rough	SE	4	SE	8	OVC	2000'
26	2936	54	Rough	E	5	E	8	OVC	1000'
27	2938	53	Rough	NE	5	NE	15-40	OVC	2500'
28	2965	54	Rough	N	4	N	5-30	OVC	3000'

* RAT ISLAND AREA

- Heavy swells.

ENCLOSURE (C)

-8-

CONFIDENTIAL

Subject: U.S.S. S-31 - Fourth War Patrol.

- -

3. Tidal Information.

The direction and velocity of currents in area MOOSE seemed consistently to follow the wind and sea. During the approach and passage of a low pressure area, the wind followed the sea with a log of about two points while the current set fairly consistently with the sea. However, during the normal weather encountered in this vicinity an average set of .5 knots to the north was experienced. On the other hand, while operating in area TIGER, and particularly while operating within ten miles to the south of the islands of TANAGA, ADAK and KAGALASKA, the direction and velocity of currents followed the tide more than they did the wind and sea. A general WSW set of 1.0 to 1.5 knots is found in close to the islands which diminishes in strength with the change in tide, and also as one progresses farther south. Strong N.E. winds and variable currents exist at the south entrance to ADAK STRAIGHT.

The above data may supplement COM HYDRO PAC #37 (142030) of September, 1942.

For R.TAN area tidal information in this vessel's third war partrol report gives a detailed resume'. There is nothing new to add.

While operating south of KISKA ISLAND, an average current of .5 knots setting 208°T was experienced in spite of heavy swells and wind from the northwest. This current varied from .2 knots during the ebb to .8 knots during the flood.

4. Navigational Aids.

Area MOOSE

In contrast to the previous patrol to the northward of the ALEUTIAN chain in July and August when stars were available for sights but once in 35 days, sights were taken about one third of all twilight periods. No land was seen at any time while in this area.

Area TIGER

U.S.C. and G.S. chart #9102 was again used for piloting while in sight of ADAK and adjacent islands. All peaks and tangents cut in accurately from NORTH CAPE on TANAGA ISLAND to TAGALAK ISLAND and they are in agreement with confidential H.O. chart #5630.

ENCLOSURE (C)

-9-

CONFIDENTIAL

Subject: U.S.S. S-31- Report of Fourth War Patrol

- -

Opportunity was again taken to cut in BOBROF, TANAGA, and GARELOI ISLANDS with respect to ADAK and GREAT SITKIN ISLANDS, which had also been done from the BERING SEA side of the chain of islands during part of the last patrol. BOBROF ISLAND is definitely 2 miles west of its plotted position on chart #9102. The 6975 foot Volcano on TANAGA ISLAND appears to be about 3 miles further to the East, as does CAPE SAJAKA; and the peak of GARELOI ISLAND appears to be about 3 miles further ESE than shown. The distance of which the southern halves of TANAGA and KANAGA ISLANDS become visible over the horizon, as computed by table 8, Bowditch, indicates clearly that both these areas are very low plateaus of about 75 feet to 150 feet altitude in spite of a 1392 foot peak shown on KANAGA ISLAND. AMATIGNAK ISLAND seems to be correctly plotted on the chart.

Area RATAK

Report of this vessel's third patrol covers all data to be reported in RATAK. Nothing new to be added except that heavy fogs at this time of year make navigation in this area exceedingly hazardous.

Area KISKA (SOUTH)

Charts U.S.C. and G.S. #9102 and H.O. Confidential Charts 5640 and 5641 were used while operating in this area. All islands and landmarks appear to be correctly plotted and positions obtained were good.

5. Ships sighted.

NONE

ENCLOSURE (C)

-10-

6. Aircraft Sighted.

DATE	TYPE	POSITION	DIST.	COURSE	ALT.	PLUS 10 TIME
8-27	PBY (1)	North of AMUKTA	2 mi.	150°T	500'	1050
8-27	B-17(1)	North of AMUKTA	2 mi.	East	300'	1240
8-28	PBY (1)	South of ATKA	3 mi.	Circling	200'	1257
9-2	Flying Bt: JAP (1)	AREA	7 Mi.	N.W.	1000'	1135
9-3	PBY (1)	AREA	8 mi.	N.E.	500'	1329
9-7	Unident	AREA	4 mi.	270°T	300'	1141
9-8	PBY (1)	AREA	8 mi.	180°T	300'	1830
9-9	PBY (1)	AREA	5 mi.	040°T	300'	1350
9-10	Unident	Area	10 mi.	WEST	500'	0725
9-10	PBY (1)	AREA	5 mi.	270°T	500'	0920
9-10	B-24 (2)	AREA	10 mi.	270°T	500'	1218
9-10	B-26 (1)	AREA	15 mi.	Cir.ADAK	1500'	1322
9-10	B-26 (1)	AREA	15 mi.	NORTH	2000'	1350
9-10	B-26 (1)	AREA	15 mi.	090°T	1000'	1407
9-10	B-24 (1)	AREA	2 mi.	180°T	2500'	1409
9-10	B-24 (1)	AREA	4 mi.	Cir090°T	1000'	1425
9-10	PBY (1)	AREA	14 mi.	090°T	1000'	1522
9-10	B-24 (2)	AREA	20 mi.	090°T	1500'	1544
9-10	B-24 (1)	AREA	20 mi.	090°T	1500'	1547
9-10	B-24 (1)	AREA	15 mi.	090°T	1000'	1625
9-10	B-24 (1)	AREA	15 mi.	090°T	1000'	1650
9-10	B-26 (1)	AREA	15 mi.	090°T	1500'	1700
9-11	PBY (1)	AREA	7 mi.	090°T	1000'	1511
9-12	PBY (1)	AREA	6 mi.	270°T	500'	0958
9-12	PBY(1)	AREA	15 mi.	090°T	1000'	1140
9-12	PBY(2)	AREA	15 mi.	270°T	1000'	1215
9-12	PBY (1)	AREA	20 mi.	030°T	1000'	1310
9-12	P-38 (2)	AREA	18 mi.	Cir.ADAK	2000'	1340
9-12	PBY (1)	AREA	20 mi.	050°T	1500'	1415
9-12	P-38 (2)	AREA	18 mi.	Cir.ADAK:	2000'	1435
9-12	P38 (2)	AREA	12 mi.	Cir.SHIP	1000'	1600
9-13	PBY (1)	AREA	15 mi.	250°T	1000'	1112
9-13	PBY (1)	AREA	15 mi.	070°T	1000'	1330
9-13	ZERO'S(2)	AREA	5 mi.	ATT.SHIP	50'	1413
9-13	Many Unid	Over KULUK BAY	20 mi.	CirKULUK	2000'	1518
9-14	PBY (1)	AREA	25 mi.	090°T	500'	1125
9-14	PBY (1)	AREA	25 mi.	090°T	500'	1138
9-14	PBY (1)	AREA	4 mi.	300°T	300'	1505
9-15	PBY (1)	AREA	15 Mi.	270°T	500'	0730
9-15	PBY (1)	AREA	15 mi.	270°T	500'	0737
9-15	PBY (1)	AREA	2 mi.	270°T	200'	1615
9-18	PBY (1)	AREA	15 mi.	200°T.	300'	1019
9-18	PBY (1)	AREA	15 mi.	020°T	200'	1350
9-19	PBY (1)	AREA	3 mi.	030°T	800'	1434
9-22	Unident	Over AMCHITKA	5 mi.	Circling CONSTAN-TINE BAY	Variab: Bombing:	1535
9-23	Unident(1)	RATAM AREA	3 mi.	000°T	300'	1057
9-23	PBY (1)	RATAM AREA	3 mi.	150°T	100'	1230
9-25	PBY (1)	South of AMCHITKA PASS	4 mi.	000°T	500'	0849

-11- ENCLOSURE (C)

CONFIDENTIAL

Subject: U.S.S. S-31 - Report of Fourth War Patrol.

8. Enemy A/S Measures.

None Observed.

9. Major defects experienced.

1. On the fourth day, leaks developed in #4 header of the stbd engine and #2 header of the port engine. In order to prevent four cylinders from flooding on a dive, these headers were drilled, valves installed, and the headers allowed to drain into the bilges continuously during a dive.

2. On the tenth day, the stbd C&R Air Compressor went out of commission and remained out of commission during the remainder of the patrol because of a cracked 1st stage cooling coil which could not be repaired at sea. The spare coil also cracked and was inreparable. The port Air Compressor 1st stage cooling coil also cracked but was repaired with a temporary copper patch. It held out until the end of the patrol.

3. Chlorine gas formed in the fwd battery compartment while attempting to run in a heavy seaway with the conning tower hatch closed, and the main and auxiliary inductions open. Sea water entered the fwd battery compartment via the auxiliary induction, drained into the fwd battery well where it apparently mixed with some residual acid. The chlorine gas was detected immediately and the proper action and precautions were taken.

4. On the twenty-third day the searchlight was put out of commission due to the breaking of our last bulb. The portable signal light is entirely unsatisfactory for long range exchange of recognition signals. The searchlight will be removed upon receipt of the Bureau type portable signalling equipment.

ENCLOSURE (C)

-12-

CONFIDENTIAL

Subject: U.S.S. S-31 - Report of Fourth War Patrol.

- -

10. Radio Reception.

Radio reception was very good. All despatches intended for us were received. However, the transmission of contact despatches to the Task Group Commander during daylight hours was very unsatisfactory. Radio equipment of S-class submarines is not suited for reliable long range transmissions during daylight hours. In three cases during this patrol when urgent messages should have been received by [illegible] or [illegible] immediately upon first transmission, a delay of two to three hours was experienced.

This vessel can usually copy [illegible] and [illegible] fairly solid at periscope depth using the loop antenna.

Last consecutive serial sent - S-31 [illegible] 260906 of September, 194[illegible].

Last consecutive serial received - C.T.G. 8.5 [illegible] 260410 of Sept., 1942.

While trying to transmit S-31's last serial to [illegible], a JAP station, closer than 500 miles estimated distance, jammed the 8270 Kc series circuit by holding his key down and we could not get the message off to [illegible]. Shifted to 4235 Kcs and transmitted to [illegible] successfully.

11. Sound Conditions and density layers.

Sound conditions were considered good although no opportunity presented itself to determine the maximum effective range or degree of receptivity.

The sound phenomena experienced by other submarines and described as a propeller beat superimposed upon a steady clicking noise was heard several times in all areas. The sound operators refer to this noise as "YEHUDI". Three times this sound was identified with whales and blackfish as noted through the periscope on the sound bearing.

No density layers were detected in any area.

ENCLOSURE (C)

-13-

CONFIDENTIAL

Subject: U.S.S. S-31 - Report of Fourth War Patrol.

- -

12. Health and Habitability.

General health of the crew was excellent. Two medical cases occurred, one of which was very serious. One man suffered a badly mutilated upper arm as a result of falling into the C&R Air Compressor lub oil pump in the motor room. The wound was liberally sprinkled with sulphanilamide and wrapped in sterile bandage. The man lost very little blood. One 1.5 cc morphine surette was administered. The man was later transferred to a PBY, which had been requested by radio. The other man suffered a deep cut on the forehead when rough seas threw him into the searchlight mount. The cut was treated with sulphatiozole salve, and it healed rapidly. One case of constipation occurred.

S-type submarines are not overly comfortable at best, but in consistently rough seas and damp weather they become very trying as far as morale is concerned.

Home-made bread, baked by the ship's cooks after regular stores ran out, was welcomed and appreciated by all hands.

ENCLOSURE (C)

-14-

CONFIDENTIAL
Subject: U.S.S. S-31 - Report of Fourth War Patrol.

- -

13. MILES STEAMED ENROUTE TO AND FROM STATION:

DATE	FROM	TO	DISTANCE	TOTAL
26-27-28 Aug.	DUTCH	--	465.0	
28 Aug - 9 Sept	- -	--	1494.0	1959
9 Sept - 20 Sept	--	--	1263.0	3222
20 Sept	--	--	80.0	3302
21 - 22 Sept.	--	--	184.0	3486
22 Sept	--	--	.0	3486
23-24 Sept	-	-	226.0	3712
24-28 Sept.			648.0	4360
TOTAL				4360

14. FUEL OIL EXPENDED

DATE	GALLONS USED	DATE	GALLONS USED
8-26	892	9-12	582
8-27	1460	9-13	700
8-28	1357	9-14	673
8-29	498	9-15	694
8-30	781	9-16	672
8-31	509	9-17	650
9-1	567	9-18	621
9-2	684	9-19	581
9-3	625	9-20	637
9-4	583	9-21	870
9-5	639	9-22	613
9-6	761	9-23	417
9-7	561	9-24	522
9-8	761	9-25	1300
9-9	787	9-26	1438
9-10	740	9-27	1720
9-11	723	9-28	724
TOTAL			25,407

-15-

ENCLOSURE (C)

CONFIDENTIAL

Subject: U.S.S. S-31 - Report of Fourth War Patrol.

15. Factors of endurance remaining.

Torpedoes - Full allowance.

Fuel - 5200 gallons

Provisions (days) Eight

Fresh water - Full tanks.

Personnel (days) Eight to Twelve.

Battery water* - 30 gallons

*Additional item which is total limiting factor for this type vessel without using double distilled potable water.

16. Factor of endurance causing end of patrol.

It appears as though all items listed under paragraph 15, except torpedoes, will be jointly responsible for bringing a patrol to an end. However, without the Kleinschmidt still, this vessel's patrol time is now limited to a maximum of 38 days because of lack of battery water. Double distilled potable water for use in the main storage battery as made by the Clarkson boiler is considered unsatisfactory except in such an emergency as having to remain on patrol for a period greater than 38 days.

17. Remarks.

1. Normal patrol procedure consisted of surface patrol during daylight hours when visibility was good and it was possible to detect planes at distances in excess of 10 miles. When visibility was such that the periscope could pick up objects at the same range as the bridge, a submerged patrol was maintained. However in the area where we were attacked by P-38's, there were so many friendly planes during days of excellent visibility that it was decided to remain on the surface and exchange recognition signals with them. PBY's and Army bombers were usually detected at ranges of 20 miles. When conducting a submerged patrol, the ship was trimmed for a one-motor normal parallel speed combination.

Batteries were invariably charged on one engine at night while making 1/3 or 2/3 on the other engine. We lay to only once to charge on both engines and that was to give the charge at a good starting rate because the battery appeared to be sluggish. An overcharge was made every five days. The battery was floated, usually at 200 amps a side in parallel, during surface patrols.

ENCLOSURE (C)

-16-

CONFIDENTIAL

Subject: U.S.S. S-31 - Report of Fourth War Patrol.

- -

A normal one-in-three watch was carried out by officers and crew. The C.O. and the second officer stood heel and toe watches of six hours duration below decks at all times in order to have a responsible coordinator for handling any emergency and to have one officer on the periscope. All hands not on watch were allowed to sleep except when a good sweep down was made daily to keep the ship clean.

2. The suggestions of the previous Commanding Officer during S-31's third war patrol in regard to alterations in S-type submarine superstructure arrangement is highly concurred in.

3. In view of the one serious medical case which occurred early in the patrol, it is again recommended that this type vessel have its personnel allowance increased to include a pharmacist's mate to replace the yeoman while the ship is at sea on patrol.

4. It is desired to replace the attack periscope (79-KA-30, #596) which is an old model, with a new periscope. The present periscope has the old 2" barrel which throws up a large feather at any speed, the index lense is in poor condition and the optical elements require overhaul.

5. It is suggested that DUTCH HARBOR be properly equipped to handle a Submarine Fox schedule for this area. A complete transmitting and receiving station should be organized which will operate within the daylight range of S-boat radio equipment so that a rapid means of delivering vital information to the local operations control center may be maintained at all times. Over two hours were recently expended by this vessel in attempting to transmit an urgent message during daylight which was finally picked up by NPC (Seattle) who is not affiliated with this communication set up.

6. In regard to the sighting and reporting of zero fighters on 13 September (page 3.), it is to be noted that the personnel who saw these planes, when interrogated after receipt of C.T.G. 8.5 despatch 141010 of September, stating that the planes were P-38's, persisted in the view that the planes were Zero's. The quartermaster saw the planes pass overhead as he was closing the hatch and he states they definitely were single tail single engine fighters. However, if the coincidental time of attack by the P-38's jibes with our time, there leaves little doubt that these men were mistaken.

ENCLOSURE (C)

-17-

1st Copy

FF12-10/A16-3(5)/ SUBMARINE FORCE, PACIFIC FLEET W1
(12)

Care of Fleet Post Office,
San Francisco, California,
December 19, 1942.

Serial 01451
DECLASSIFIED.
CONFIDENTIAL

Reg. No. 6310
R.S. No. 1 0224

COMSUBPAC PATROL REPORT NO. 110
U.S.S. S-31 - FIFTH WAR PATROL.

From: The Commander Submarine Force, Pacific Fleet.
To : Submarine Force, Pacific Fleet.

Subject: U.S.S. S-31 (SS136) - Report of Fifth War Patrol. 19 Oct 1942 - 7 Nov. 1942

Enclosure: (A) Copy of ComTaskGroup 8.5 Conf ltr TG8.5/A16-3 Serial 043 of November 14, 1942.
(B) Copy of Comsubron 45 Conf ltr FC5-45/A16-3 Serial 056 of November 14, 1942.
(C) Copy of Subject War Patrol.

1. The Commanding Officer covered his area thoroughly and exhibited aggressiveness in his attack on the 3,000 ton mine layer. In this connection, the remarks of Commander Task Group 8.5 in paragraph 5 are concurred in.

2. The U.S.S. S-31 is congratulated on having inflicted the following damage on the enemy:

SUNK

1 Mine Layer (CM) - 3,000 tons.

R. H. ENGLISH.

DISTRIBUTION
(35CM-42)
List III: SS.
Special:
P1(5), EN3(5), Z1(5),
Consublant (2), X3(1),
Consubsowespac (2),
Sub. School, N.L. (2).

E.R. Swinburne
E.R. SWINBURNE,
Flag Secretary.

COMMANDER IN CHIEF U.S. FLEET RECEIVED

FILMED

44816 FILMED

TC8.5/A16-3
Serial 043

November 14, 1942.

CONFIDENTIAL

From: The Commander Task Group Eight Point Five.
To : The Commander Submarine Force, Pacific Fleet.

Subject: U.S.S. S-31 - Report of Fifth War Patrol.

Enclosure: (A) Original and one copy of subject report.
(B) Copy of Reconnaissance Report.

1. Although but thirteen days of this twenty-nine day patrol were spent in assigned patrol areas, twenty-two were spent in waters used by enemy shipping.

2. The patrol was characterized by intelligent planning and resolute execution. The estimates set forth in the report are indicative of an understanding of the problems presented and mature judgment in their solution.

3. The reason given for preparing a more voluminous patrol report than is ordinarily necessary is concurred in. Reconnaissance of enemy territory resulted in the collection of valuable information, a separate report of which has been made, Enclosure (B).

4. The decision not to attack a minor target on the night of October 30, while taking position to intercept three cruisers is approved. In connection with the attempted interception of these important targets, consideration should have been given to a surface patrol to increase its effectiveness.

5. The attack on a mine-layer on October 26 was boldly carried through to a successful conclusion. It is considered the S-31 should be credited with sinking one 3000-ton mine-layer. The retirement after the attack was skillfully accomplished under difficult circumstances.

6. By copy hereof the Task Group Commander congratulates the Commanding Officer, officers and crew of the S-31 on a well conducted patrol and on the damage inflicted upon the enemy.

ENCLOSURE (A)

FC45/A16-3
Serial 056

November 14, 1942.

CONFIDENTIAL

From: The Commander Submarine Squadron Forty-Five.
To : The Commander Submarine Force, Pacific Fleet.

Subject: U.S.S. S-31 - Fifth War Patrol.

1. The Fifth War Patrol of the S-31 covered a period of twenty-seven (27) days, of which ten (10) days were spent on station. Enroute to and from the patrol area enemy shipping routes were also patrolled. Fuel was the factor terminating this patrol. The distance to the area patrolled, fifteen hundred and fifty (1550) miles, is approximately the limiting distance to which the S-Class submarines can be effectively used.

2. The S-31 returned in excellent material condition and was able to proceed to San Diego for scheduled upkeep after three (3) days in port. Only two defects reported are considered major. These were the casualties to the regulator tank and to the starboard C&R air compressor. All defects will be corrected during the upkeep period.

3. Commander Submarine Squadron Forty-Five congratulates the Commanding Officer, officers, and crew on a well conducted patrol.

ENCLOSURE (B)

CONFIDENTIAL

Subject: U.S.S. S-31 - Report of Fifth War Patrol

PROLOGUE - Arrived DUTCH HARBOR on September 28, 1942, from Fourth War Patrol. Commenced refit on September 29, 1942, by Submarine Base personnel assisted by ship's force. Completed refit on October 12, 1942. Normal repairs; no alterations, U.S.S. S-34 TAR motor-generator installed; ours installed in U.S.S. S-32. Readiness for sea on October 13, 1942, not depermed or wiped. No training period.

1. NARRATIVE

October 13, 1942 (W)
Underway singly on patrol mission in accordance C.T.G. 8.5 Operation order 23-42 of October 13, 1942. Mission to patrol area , intercepting, attacking and destroying enemy forces encountered. 1900 Cleared AKUTAN PASS.

October 14, 1942 (X)
0702 Made trim dive; continuing to area; seas rough, wind from North.

October 15, 1942 (Y)
0608 Made dawn dive. Exercised crew at emergency drills and stations submerged.

October 16, 1942 (Y)
0530 Made dawn dive. Exercised crew at emergency drills and battle stations submerged. Made battle surface; fired five (5) rounds from 4"/50 gun; fired one pan each from Thompson submachine guns Browning rifle and Lewis machine gun. (See paragraph 10 for casualty during firing) 1215 Received word that 2 enemy DDs are headed this way, probably to rendezvous with a Maru in lower KISKA -- and --. CACHALOT in that area but probably submerged close in and not cognizant of situation. My course and speed should intercept in lower KISKA -- around 2200 tonite if Maru not picked up by DDs. 1400 Received word DDs heading for North of BOODLE, Zigzagging at high speed - tough luck, we might have made contact.
1500 Crossed 180th meridian. Commenced zigzagging on surface during daylight hours for duration of patrol.

October 18, 1942 (M)
0538 Made dawn dive. Passed point 63, heading for area. Received word Army planes got the 2 DDs.

October 19, 1942 (M)
0618 Made dawn dive. 1725 Made evening dive. Will enter area tomorrow p.m.

October 20, 1942 (L)
0528 Made dawn dive. Entered area; commenced patrolling at 2/3 speed on one engine, surface patrol. Best cover-

-1-

ENCLOSURE (C)

CONFIDENTIAL

Subject: U.S.S. S-31 - Report of Fifth War Patrol.

- -

age of possible enemy speeds and courses appears to be on east-west patrol line. 1713 Made evening dive.

October 21, 1942 (L)
0527 Made dawn dive. 1710 Made evening dive. Weather excellent for surface patrol.

October 22, 1942 (L)
0527 Made dawn dive. 1500 Received C.T.G. 8.5 directing us proceed to PARAMUSHIRU. 1530 c/c/ to 247°, both engines ahead 2/3. Will adjust speed to be off SHIMUSHU by dawn the 24th (L). 1727 Made evening dive. 1800 Departed area. Regulating tank out of commission (see paragraph 10).

October 24, 1942(L)
0540 Made dawn dive. My patrol Plan at Present is as follows: Arrive off east coast PARAMUSHIRU at dawn 24th(L) conduct submerged patrol in neighborhood of HIGASHIBANJO SUIDO trying to ascertain if, KASHIWABARA WAN is departure point of enemy ships for ALEUTIAN AREA, attacking and destroy any such shipping encountered; thereafter proceeding southward along the shore line, reconnoitering MUSASHI WAN, thence eastward and northward to KUJIRA WAN on east coast of PARAMUSHIRU. Will maintain patrol until fuel consideration or expenditure of torpedoes dictates return to base. Destroyed certain registered publications in accordance with SUBPACFLT Conf. ltr. 1-42 of January 18, 1942. 1720 Made evening dive. 2100 Increased speed to standard in order to arrive off HIGASHIBANJO SUIDO by dawn. <u>Gave crew lecture on what to do if taken prisoner; reviewed "scuttle ship" bill</u>. 2400 entered area ________.

October 24, 1942 (K)
Apparently my tentative patrol plan is satisfactory; intercepted S-32 saying good hunting on east coast PARAMUSHIRU from HIGASHIBANJO SUIDO to MUSASHI WAN. Also received C.T.G. 8.5 TOTEM BAY. Destroyed E.C.M. and attendant publications. 0450 Made quick dive on course 250°T. Conducting submerged patrol off HIGASHIBANJO SUIDO. Watered battery. Depth Control difficult; gale blowing from S.W. No shipping sighted. 1740 Surfaced on course 260°T. Full moon. Position doubtful. Sighted reefs on port bow, distance ½ mile c/c to right. Sighted more reefs on port beam; c/c to

-2- ENCLOSURE "C"

CONFIDENTIAL

Subject: U.S.S. S-31 - Report of Fifth War Patrol.

- -

right. Apparently we surfaced in HIGASHIBANJO SUIDO entrance; S.W. gale set us to northward more than we had allowed. This demonstrates the absolute necessity for a fathometer. However, patrol today covered both northeast and southeast approaches to HIGASHIBANJO SUIDO.

October 25, 1942(K)
Received C.T.G. 8.5 "DEEP INLET". 0504 Made quick dive. Patrolled area NISHIBANJO SUIDO to T.T.MIGHI YAMA along 20 fathom curve. No shipping. Two houses at YOTSUIWA. There are apparently two good stretches of beach suitable for landings between MATYA ZAKI, both at the mouth of small rivers. The southerly river has a small reef just north of its mouth - MITSUKOSHI I.A. - about 1/4 mile off shore. The rest of the coast line seems fairly rocky. Having difficulty identifying peaks for navigational fixes. 1740 Surfaced; covered with glass balls- must have ran through a fishing net. Brilliant moon; steering into moonpath all night, describing circle to southward while charging batteries. Ten to twelve miles off shore and in shipping lane to northeast of ONEKOTAN PASS.

October 26, 1942 (K)
0447 Sighted sodium flare or light bearing 345°T. Dived thinking it was sampan close aboard. Sound heard no screws, however, and light disappeared. From bearings after daylight, determined light to be on hill behind OTOMAYE. 0825 Sighted unidentified ship in OTOMAYE WAN. Battle stations submerged; commenced approach. 0922 Fired two torpedoes at a modified O.IMOSHIMA type mine layer. Two hits. Ship sank at anchorage. 0923 went aground on reef. 0925 went aground at 30 foot keel depth. Backed off; went ahead. 0927 What appeared to be the bow wave of a surfacing torpedo was observed to pass about 700 yards astern. 0928 to 0955 Went aground several times at periscope depth. 1000 Reached deep water. No A/S measures. Retired to southeast to give everyone a rest. Reloaded tubes. Inspected ship for any damage due to grounding; none apparent at present time. 1725 Surfaced. It is believed that, due to the extensive building program which has been carried out at OTOMAYE, this is one of the points from which enemy shipping departs for the ALEUTIAN AREA. In view of the fact that the south end of PARAMUSHIRU is probably a hornet's nest right now, will vary my strategy a bit and head for KARUMABETSU WAN tonight in order to strike at separated points rather than at MUSASHI WAN which is adjacent to OTOMAYE WAN. Making passage of ONEKOTAN STRAIGHT tonight. No coast patrol encountered as yet. Very rough seas.

Contact #1

-3- ENCLOSURE "C"

CONFIDENTIAL

Subject: U.S.S. S-31 - Report of Fifth War Patrol.

- -

October 27, 1942 (K)
Encountered monstrous seas in ONEKOTAN PASS. Gyro went out (see paragraph 10) magnetic variations in this locality are so changeable that Coast Pilot recommends extra-careful navigation, C.O.C. bilges full of water, #1 periscope motor grounded, H.P. pump too hot to run on C.O.C. bilges, and trim pump strainer clogging so often that it is difficult to make headway with the pumping. In addition to this, had to dive at dawn since we were close in to MUSASHI WAN; 8000 lbs. heavy [illegible] bilges full. Depth control bad. Maintaining submerged patrol 60-70 feet with periscope exposures every half hour. Battery very low at noon because of speed to hold depth. 1745 Surfaced. Logistics: When #3 MBT goes dry, will have 1800 gallons fuel oil for "on station" patrol, leaving enough for return trip at 8 knots with 2000 gallons reserve. Will have to leave on November 1, or 2nd.

October 28, 1942 (K)
0500 Made quick dive. Reconnoitering from NAGAI[illegible] ZAKI to KAKUMABETSU WAN which is reported to be a Naval base. Patrolling 20-50 fathom curve; got good look into bay. No ships. Several houses on beach which form a fishing village, and two larger buildings or storage houses on DIAGO ZAKI. Continued south to KUJIRA WAN, no ships in bay there. Good sized fishing village; no new installations. Water on west side PARAMUSHIRU not as deep as charted. Landings could easily be made at either KUJIRA WAN or KAKUMABETSU WAN. Certainly expected to sight something today. Looks like west side of island is non-military. 1740 Surfaced. Water like glass all day; short periscope exposures.

October 29, 1942(K)
Proceeding to MUSASHI WAN. 0500 Made quick dive. 1210

Contact #2 Sighted large supply vessel anchored inside MUSASHI WAN. In view of S-32 experience here and our own experience in OTOMAYE WAN, remaining well outside 18 fathom curve. Will have to wait until he leaves to get him. Reconnoitered MUSASHI WAN from south and east. Many houses on beach; one large white building similar to one sighted at OTOMAYE WAN (see paragraph 3 under "Remarks"); Light house on KURABU ZAKI with houses around base; some sort of towers to north of light house; six large hangars, three of which may be barracks, indicating that there is an air base here (we have not seen a single plane); and several houses at KAISHA.

-4- ENCLOSURE "C"

CONFIDENTIAL

Subject: U.S.S. S-31 - Report of Fifth War Patrol.
- -

October 29, 1942 (K) (Cont)
Contact #3 1530 Sighted light mine layer of SHIMUSHU or NATSUSHIMA
class rounding KURABU ZAKI proceeding into MUSASHI WAN.
He must have come down the coast close in to the beach;
I did not sight him until he was 6 miles astern. Will
lay for him tomorrow. He is apparently patrolling during
daylight between OTOMAYE WAN and MUSASHI WAN. 1736 Surfaced. MUSASHI WAN appears to be the largest Naval base
on PARAMUSHIRU; OTOMAYE WAN is next in size - these op-
inions from a periscope point of view. ALEUTIAN traffic
undoubtedly originates at these two ports, which seem
to be protected by underwater reefs and shoals. Weather
is still holding fair. 2200 Sighted orange (sodium)
flare over the horizon bearing 225°T. This bearing
passes through KUROISHI WAN on ONEKOTAN TO, so there may
be some activity there. Received C.T.G. 8.5
saying S-31 has area ____, which we are now in. Set #3
and #4 torpedoes for two feet; NATSUSHIMA type CM draws
but 5 feet 9 inches.

October 30, 1942 (K)
Patrolling on surface covering ONEKOTAN PASS. 0510
Made quick dive. Covering MUSASHI WAN, waiting for AK or
Contact #4 CM to come out. 1030 Sighted HOJIMA type AK rounding
KURABU ZAKI and standing in to MUSASHI WAN. He was
five miles away. 1050 AK anchored. There are now two AKs
and one CM in MUSASHI WAN. If it were not for the 40
foot shoal two miles from the beach, I could get at them.
However, minimum firing range without grounding is not
less than 3500 yards. Better to wait. Spent afternoon
patrolling 20 fathom curve and locating shore installations. Stayed in close to KURABU ZAKI until dark in
hopes a ship would leave MUSASHIWAN. 1800 Surfaced.
1930 Received C.T.G. 8.5 GRANT COVE. 2000 c/c to 055°T
speed 2/3 on one to gain best interception point (see
Contact #5 brief estimate of situation following narrative). 2148
Sighted unidenfied vessel broad on port bow, distance
4000 yards, course 080°T, speed 15 knots, silhouetted
against the moon. Went to night attack stations, a pure-
ly defensive measure at this time since we do not want
to divulge our position. Appeared to be the SHIMUSHU
or NATSUSHIMA type CM which was in MUSASHI WAN today.
Believe he is on way to rendezvous with enemy force
approaching PARAMUSHIRU. Closest range was about 3500
yards. 2230 Secured from night attack stations; secured
tubes. Radar here would have been very useful. It also
appears, from this incident, that SHIMUSHU type CMs
either

-5- ENCLOSURE "C"

CONFIDENTIAL

Subject: U.S.S. S-31 - Report of Fifth War Patrol.

October 30, 1942 (K) (Cont)
do not have radar or supersonic gear, or they do not use them in their own waters.

October 31, 1942 (K)
Contact #6 0257 Sighted unidentifed ship crossing from starboard to port distance 2000 yards. Went to night attack stations. O.O.D. turned with enemy instead of against, thus making us the hub of rotation for enemy turning circle. He was circling on station, apparently awaiting approach of CLs. This indicates I am on right track for interception. Believe I could have made a possible hit on this target since #3 and #4 torpedoes were set at 2 feet. He was our old friend of a few hours ago, I think; a SHIMUSHU or NATSUSHIMA type CM. He did not detect us or he would have undoubtedly opened fire at that range. Finally got him astern and went to standard speed to open the range. 0335 Secured from attack stations. 0500 arrived at interception spot; made quick dive; patrolling on enemy course line, covering speeds of advance from 12-20 knots. 1630 Reversed course, returning to MUSASHI WAN. 1745 Surfaced - Although it is very disappointing that we did not sight the CLs, the action taken to intercept is considered strategically sound within the limitations of S-type Submarines.

November 1, 1942 (K)
0500 Made quick dive. Approaching MUSASHI WAN. One AK ther this morning. The other, which was in a light condition, has apparently left for the south. Sea like
Contact #7 glass, slight swell. 0957 Sighted SHIMUSHU type CM bearing 120°T distance 3 miles course 200°T.. Went to battle stations; commenced approach. Got ready #3 and #4 tubes which have torpedoes set for two feet. Upon closer observation of this vessel, my opinion changes. He is not a CM. He is a new gunboat. His silhouette is very similar to SHIMUSHU type CM but he has a flush deck fore and aft where CM has broken deck at forecastle. 1140 Discontinued approach; PG entered harbor and we almost grounded over 18 fathom curve at KURABU SAKI. (see paragraph 7) Secured from battle stations; continued patrol. 1730 Surfaced. Set course to clear area. Received C.T.G. 8.5 JADSHI COVE. Will answer tomorrow night so S-35 can replace us. Believe DOLPHIN will be well clear to south of us by tomorrow. Port air compressor first stage cooling coil ruptured again - considered irreparable this time. (see paragraph 10)

-6- ENCLOSURE "C"

CONFIDENTIAL

Subject: U.S.S. S-31 - Report of Fifth War Patrol.

- -

November 2, 1942 (K) to November 6, 1942 (Y) inclusive.

Proceeding to Base, making morning and evening dives, zig-zagging on surface with a 90% ZZ plan, going ahead 2/3 on both engines, carrying a 150-200 amp a side parallel float. 2200 /2(L) Departed area ______. 0030 /3(L) Attempting to transmit my **EAST CLUMP** but transmitter will not put out. M.C. set is fine, but H.F. side of TBR is out somewhere. Want to get this despatch off so S-35 can move in to good area. Too far to get DUTCH on 450 Kcs. 2200 /3(L) Attempting to transmit my EAST CLUMP. TBR will still not radiate although have been working on it. Believe trouble is with antenna now (see paragraph 10). East winds and seas from east permit us to make about 6.4 knots average speed. Very heavy seas. 2230 /4(L) Cleared my EAST CLUMP to C.T.G. 8.5 via CINCPAC. Too much interference with NPC. 0130 /5(L) Starboard air compressor out of commission (see paragraph 10). 2015 /5(L) Cleared my FROG ROCK to C.T.G. 8.5 2130 /5(L) Received C.T.G. 8.5 KELP BAY and LATE POINT. Received C.T.F. 8 042336 of November 2200 /6(L) Received CINCPAC 060535 of November. Seas making up very heavy from east. Wind becoming strong, shifting to South. 0700/7(L) Passed Point 63. Heavy seas from S.W. 2000 /6(Y) Crossed 180th Meridian. 2031 /6(Y) Transmitted my GIG PASS to C.T.G.8.5.

November 7, 1942 (Y)

0210 Received C.T.G. 8.5 MARBLE BAY.

Contact #8 — 0812 Sighted large unidentified submarine bearing 230°T on identical course distance 5 miles, overtaking. Dived. Battle stations submerged. Commenced approach. Distant explosions; rigged for depth charge attack - sixteen charges in all; closest estimated at 6000 yards. Saw other submarine once after diving as we were changing course to close him. He must have dived immediately after my observation because I did not see him again. Submarine could have been CACHALOT, but I have no definite information concerning his return to DUTCH; therefore assume him to be enemy. Depth charges seem to bear me out; they must have come from U.S. aircraft at LONGVIEW. However, I saw no planes at any time, and I'm positive no surface craft were present. Believe we were not sighted by submarine. In view of unusual circumstances will carry out submerged search-patrol for enemy submarine during day. 1100 Secured from Battle stations. If other submarine was CACHALOT she will get contact report off; if not CACHALOT, aircraft will probably report bombing or depth charging. 1745 Cleared my HELM ROCK to C.T.G. 8.5.

-7- ENCLOSURE "C"

CONFIDENTIAL

Subject: U.S.S. S-31 - Report of Fifth War Patrol.

- -

November 8, 1942 (Y) to November 10, 1942 (W)

Enroute base, making morning and evening dives. 0100 /8(Y) Passed Point 65. Seas choppy. 0130 /8(X) Cleared AMUKTA PASS. Cleared by ICY STRAIT to C.T.G. 8.5 Received C.T.G. 8.5 ORCA ISLAND. Seas very heavy from north. Weather overcast. 1120 /9(x) Sighted two PBYs on northeast course. Passed within 1 1/2 miles, but no recognition. 1600 /9(x) Passed POINT 66. 2300 /9(X) Received C.T.G. 8.5 PEACOCK ISLAND. 0930 /10(W) Arrived DUTCH HARBOR.

Brief estimate of situation after receipt of C.T.G. 8.5 GIANT COVER on 10-30-42.

1. Information.

At 0030(Z) today, thirtieth, three enemy cruisers of the NAGARA class and one DD were sighted in Latitude 52-53N, Longitude 168-09E, speed 15 knots, course 250°T, which course is direct to KURABU ZAKI. C.T.G. 8.5 despatch received at 1930 (K). At 2030 (K) this vessel in Latitude 49-50N, Longitude 155-39E. Instructions are to intercept the enemy force.

Assumption.

(1) That the enemy will hold course for MUSASHI WAN, but may vary speed between twelve and twenty knots.

(2) That the enemy has no definite information of our present position although he knows that a submarine has been in the vicinity.

(3) That the enemy will probably send out antisubmarine escorts for this force.

(4) That the sea and the weather will be favorable for a daylight periscope attack.

(5) That air coverage will be furnished to the enemy.

2. Decision.

This vessel will intercept and destroy, insofar as possible, units of the subject enemy force.

3. Course of action.

This vessel will be in such a position at 0500 (K) that contact will be made with the enemy at daylight if he is making a speed of twenty knots; or, if he is making fifteen knots, contact will be established by 1630 (K) by S-31 moving to a position during daylight eighteen miles on enemy reverse course from 0500 (K) position; and, if contact is not made with the enemy at either of those times, S-31 will retire on the surface during the night on enemy course making contact at 0530 (K) the following morning if the enemy makes twelve knots good. In any event, if contact is not established, another reconnaissance of MUSASHI WAN will be made in order to obtain positive or negative information of the presence of enemy cruisers there.

-8- ENCLOSURE "C"

CONFIDENTIAL

Subject: U.S.S. S-31 - Report of Fifth War Patrol.

The one real disadvantage of this plan is that S-31 cannot cover enemy possible courses.

X. General. Normal submerged patrol procedure. Torpedoes set at six feet. Remain undetected by enemy coast patrols, escorts and and planes. Plane up to forty feet every half hour in order to utilize maximum radius of submerged visibility. Reload as rapidly as possible in order to get in a second attack.

Brief estimate of situation after receipt of C.T.G. 8.5 GRANT COVE on 10-30-42 (Cont).

4. Logistics.

This vessel has fuel for two more days on station, allowing for the necessary reserve for return to home base.

5. Basic Plants, etc.

Minus ten zone time.

-9- ENCLOSURE "C"

2. WEATHER

Below is a tabulated record of the weather encountered during the patrol. It may be of aerological interest to future operations.

Date	Barometer	Temp.	Sea	Force	Wind	Force	Visibility	Miles	Ceiling	Sky
Enroute Station.										
October 13	2975	46	Rough	8	N	8	Fair	2-10	0	Clear-Snow.
14	2994	49	Choppy	3	N	2	Good	25	3000	Ptly-ovc.
15	3009	49	Choppy	2	NW	2	Exollent	U	U	Clear
16	3004	50	Calm	2	SE	2	Excellent	U	2500	ovc.
18	3015	50	Choppy	2	NE	2	Excellent	U	3000	Ovc..
19	3057	49	Swells	1	W	2	Excellent	U	30000	Ptrl-ovc.
20	3016	50	Rough	3	SW	4	Good	3-U	2000	Ovc.
21	2990	50	Rough	3	SW	3	Excellent	U	30000	U.
22	3001	51	Rough	3	W	2	Excellent	U	30000	U.
Enroute PARAMUSHIRU										
23	3007	50	Calm	1	SW	1	Excellent	U	30000	U.
24	2980	48	Gale	8	SW	8	Poor	2-3	1000	Ovc.
25	2957	48	Choppy	2	SW	1	Excellent	U	30000	U
26	2967	44	Choppy	3	W	2	Good	10	30000	Ptly-ovc.
27	2995	44	Heavy Swells	3	W	3	Excellent	U	30000	U .
28	3001	47	Calm	1	0	1	Excellent	U	30000	U .
29	2994	46	Swells	1	SW	2	Excellent	U	30000	U.
30	3007	43	Swells	1	SW	1	Good	25	5000	Ovc.
31	3006	43	Choppy	1	SW	1	Fair	3-20	3000	Ovc.
NOVEMBER										
1	3004	44	Glassy	0	C	0	Excellent	U	30000	U.
2	3008	41	Rough	3	W	3	Excellent	U	30000	U.
Enroute DUTCH HARBOR										
3	2986	43	Rough	3	SE	3	Poor	5	2000	Ovc.
4.	2983	47	Rough	3	E	3	Poor	5	2000	Ovc.
5	3011	49	Rough	3	SSW	3	Poor	8	500	Ovc.
6	3022	49	Rough	4	SE	5	Poor	8	500	Ovc.
6	2952	47	Rough	4	SW	4	Poor	10	500	Ovc.
7	2953	48	Swells	3	W	2	Fair	5-20	3000	Ptly-ovc.
8	2947	44	Rough	4	NW	4	Poor	4	1000	Ovc.
9	2951	43	Rough	4	N	4	Poor	5-10	1000	Ovc.
10	2956	43	Choppy	2	NW	3	Fair	5-15	1000	Ovc.

ENCLOSURE "C"

-10-

<u>CONFIDENTIAL</u>

Subject: U.S.S. S-31 - Report of Fifth War Patrol.

- -

2. WEATHER (continued)

As is indicated from the table, the weather was usually and surprisingly clear in the PARATTU and PARAMUSHIRO areas for the greater part of the time. This bears out the Coast Pilot which states that the months of September and October are the two clear months during the later half of the year. The weather during the return trip, however, was very unfavorable. Two men were injured due to heavy seas.

3. TIDAL INFORMATION.

No abnormal currents or tides were encountered. The currents close in to PARAMUSHIRU TO are as shown on H.O chart 5322, but are negligible at five to ten miles offshore exept in ONEKOTAN KAIKYO where a one half knot current sets northwest and southeast through the center of the pass. In close to KURABU ZAKI and KAPARI ZAKI strong currents were observed at maximum flood and ebb although sufficient data could not be obtained while submerged to compute the force of these currents. A rough estimate is around two knots.

On several occasions, it was observed that the times of slack water close in to the above mentioned points were about two hours after the times of L.W. and H.W. at the nearest reference point, CAPE LOPATKA, on the KAMCHATKA pennisula.

4. NAVIGATIONAL AIDS

The tops of jagged mountains were used to obtain navigational fixes for the greater part of the time. However, it was clear 90% of the time and stars could have been used. The mountain tops cut in very well on H.O chart 5322, but low lying tangent of headlands and points should be accepted under suspicion. Due to the changing coast line of this island, it is believed that some points of land are in error as much as a half mile.

Ships navigating the waters around PARAMUSHIRU who are equipped with depth finding gear should consider H.O chart 5322 in error by at least two fathoms less than shown.

There is a prominent control tower or lighthouse with an outside spiral ladder, located about a quarter of a mile north of the tip of KURABU ZAKI at MUSASHI WAN. Irregular flashes have been observed from this tower and surrounding buildings at night.

Many submerged rocks whose presence is denoted only by swells and on occasional spray will be found off HIGASHI BANJO SUIDO.

The Coast Pilot states that there is evidence of all the KURIL ISLANDS gradually rising from the sea. Uncharted shoals found on OTOMAYE WAN, and also reported in MUSASHI WAN,

- 11 - ENCLOSURE (C)

CONFIDENTIAL

Subject: U,S.S. S-31 - Report of Fifth War Patrol.

- -

might indicate that in some places PARAMUSHIRU TO has risen some forty to fifty feet in the last twenty five years. In fact, the small island northeast of ARAIDO TO has progressed from shoal water to an elevation of 439 feet since the JAPANESE Coast Pilot was printed.

The bubble octant recently acquired by this vessel did not undergo a proper test on this patrol because the navigator was more interested in improving his ability with the conventional sextant at night. No sights were taken earlier than a full hour after evening twilight or an hour before dawn. Considerable improvement in night sights resulted from the use of the light filters to reduce a star's brilliance on a very dim horizon. Night fixex, thus obtained, were never in error more than ten miles. The bubble octant fix obtained during the only opportunity when the sea was calm enough to use it, was 75 miles out. In view of the fact that a 25 mile error is considered satisfactory, it is felt that the time and energy required to become proficient in the use of this instrument is entirely out of proportion to its usefulness to any vessel that keeps a careful D.R.

5. DESCRIPTION OF ENEMY SHIPS SIGHTED.

Contact	Date&Time	Position	Course	Speed	Description
1	10-26-42 0825(K)	Lat.50-09N Long.155-37E	-	-	Similar to OKINOSHIMA type mine layer; Clipper bow, counter stern mid-ship island, one large stack tripod mainmast, stick foremast ahead of bridge structure, protected guns fore & aft, mine gear aft, estimated tonnage 3000 tons.
2.	10-29-42 1210(K)	Lat.50-01N Long.155-21E	-	-	Replica of NOJIMA type AK.
3.	10-29-42 1530(K)	Lat.49-59N Long.144-25E	Var.	8	Replica of SHIMUSHU or NATSUSHIMA type CM
4.	10-30-42 1050(K)	Lat.49-59N Long.155-26E	Var.	5	NOJIMA type AK
5.	10-30-42 2146(K)	Lat.49-55N Long.155-48E	075°T	15	Definitely SHIMUSH type CM
6.	10-31-42	Lat.50-05N Long.156-29E	335°T	8	Same as SHIMUSHU type CM as above.

- 12 -

ENCLOSURE (C)

CONFIDENTIAL

Subject: U.S.S. S-31 - -Report of Fifth War Patrol.

- -

Contact	Date&Time	Position	Course	Speed	Description
7.	11-1-42 0957(K)	Lat.49-56N Long.155-22E	200°T	12	New type gunboat very similar to our large PC boats. Silhouette is almost the same. Flush deck; estimated size guns; 2-4.7", one forward, one aft; depth charges on stern; raked bow; square stern; single raked stack. Estimated 2000 Tons.
8.	11-7-42 0812(Y)	Lat.50-43N Long.177-23W	086°T	10	Fleet type submarine (Later identified as CACHALOT).

6. AIRCRAFT SIGHTED.

Date	Type	No.	Position	Course	Alt.	Dist.	Time
10/14	PBY	1	South UMNAK	230°T	500 ft.	30 Mi.	0750(X)
10/14	PBY	1	South UMNAK	045°T	500 ft.	20 Mi.	0919(X)
10/14	PBY	1	South UMNAK	225°T	500 ft.	15 Mi.	0922(X)
11/9	PBY	2	North AMUKTA	045°T	800 ft.	20 Mi.	1120(X)

- 13 - ENCLOSURE (C)

CONFIDENTIAL

Subject: U.S.S. S-31 - Report of Fifth War Patrol

7. SUMMARY OF SUBMARINE ATTACKS

Paragraph (7)

	1.	
Attack	Periscope	
Date	10-28-42	
Location Lat.	50-10N	
Location Long.	155-36E	
Torpedoes fired on each attack	2	
Hits	2	
Number Sunk (Tonnage)	3000	
Number Damaged or probably sunk		
Type of Target	Mine Layer	
Range 1500 yards or less.		
Range more than 1500 yards	2400	
Periscope Depth	45'	
Surface Night		
Deep Submergence		
Estimated Draft Target	14'	
Torpedo Depth Setting	6'	
Bow or Stern Shot	Bow	
Track Angle	100 P	
Gyro Angle	0	
Estimated Speed Target	0	
Firing Interval	20"	
Spread - Amount & King	Longitudinal; point of aim was stack & stern	

Remarks: This vessel was anchored in about five fathoms of water in OTOMAYE WAN. The firing range was excessive because of the approach of the submarine in shallow water as noted by the C.O.

- 14 - ENCLOSURE (C)

CONFIDENTIAL

Subject: U.S.S. S-31 - Report of Fifth War Patrol.

CONTACT #1

At 0830 (K) on October 2 ,1942, an unidentified ship was sighted a half a point forward of the starboard beam, distance about six miles, close in to the shore. Weather was clear, sea calm, and a bright sun was low in the sky to seaward of us. Battle stations were manned and the approach was started. I did not know exactly what kind of a ship it was, although it had been reported by the periscope watch officer as a tanker. Neither did I know how far off the beach the ship was or if I could get within a reasonable firing range. I had instructions to stay outside the 18 fathom curve. Upon closer approach to this vessel, it appeared she was underway because her bearing was changing slowly to port and smoke was coming from her stack. It also appeared at that time that a fairly good firing range of about 1500 yards could be obtained, so the attack was pressed home. As the range decreased to 3600 yards, I could feel, or sense, by the motion of the ship, that we were passing over shoal water even though brief bearings on land tangents still placed us outside the 18 fathom curve. Further study of the vessel indicated that she was a large mine layer similar to the OKINOSHIMA class but somewhat lighter. Her superstructure, as later determined by comparison to ONI 14, was much like the OKINOSHIMA less the aircraft, but her hull had a clipper bow rather than the OKINOSHIMA cruiser bow. Also, she was anchored, port side to us, and what had made it a pear that she was underway was actually our own bearing changing to starboard due to a fairly strong northerly set. The target, being my first, was too tempting at that range, so we continued to inch in at slow speed. If we had touched bottom at any time during the approach, the attack would have been discontinued. Short periscope observations showed a large settlement on the shore, apparently no other large shipping in the vicinity, and no air coverage for the area. At 0922, fired #1 and #2 tubes with a twenty second firing interval, on a 100° port track, zero gyro angles, zero firing bearing. Range at firing was estimated to be between 2000 and 2500 yards; however, I did not feel bound to approach any closer due to the apparent shallowness of the water. By fix, we fired on the 18 fathom curve and we should have had plenty of water, but due to the chart inaccuracies and age of survey (1914) the soundings were incorrect. Immediately after firing #2, we scraped bottom pulling normal series parallel with full right rudder just coming on. A minute later we bumped

- 15 - ENCLOSURE (C)

CONFIDENTIAL

Subject: U.S.S. S-31 - Report of Fifth War Patrol.

- -

bottom again at 40 feet. One can imagine my consternation at this time wondering if our turning circle would put me in shallower or deeper water. Two minutes after firing we heard one torpedo explosion followed shortly thereafter by the other. Recorded times cannot be depended on because of the high tension and strained minds in the control room at this time, but the run of torpedoes indicated an average firing range of 2400 yards. A half minute after hearing the explosions we grounded and stopped in 30 feet of water, and I took this doubtful opportunity to see what the target looked like and what, if any, A/S measures were forthcoming from the enemy. Apparently two hits had demolished the stern of the target since she was already half submerged and down by the stern with an angle of about 30°. No A/S measures yet even though our conning tower was out of water and we were stopped (visions of TOKYO prison for the duration). Tried backing down while I was looking - moved a little - kicked her ahead - slid over the reef and making headway again - down to 39 feet. Took another periscope look - astern of us was what looked like the bow wave of a torpedo finishing a surface run, range about 700 yards. No other activity and the target was still visible with bow well out of water but water covering after superstructure up to stack. For the next twenty minutes we were scraping from one reef to another. Everytime I began to think we were in the clear and tried to get down to 50 feet, we would bump again and bounce up to 40 feet. By now we were going ahead series-series in order not to damage the boat any more than possible which would certainly have been done using high speed. During this period, a much regretted periscope exposure showed white breakers notmore than fifty yards away on our port side. There is no sensation quite like that obtained when twisting and turning, trying to stay at periscope depth, searching for a path through the reefs to deep water. Finally at 0955 we dropped off into deep water again. It is believed that the forward motion of the ship at high speed and the submerged turning circle had combined to put us well inside the 15 fathom curve and to the northward on the reefs which are not plotted on the chart. The reason that no complete A/S measures were taken by the enemy is not readily apparent. The closest reported air base, located 12 miles south of this bay, was covered by a heavy snow storm during our escape, as was the Naval base there. Probably that is why surface ships and aircraft did not take after us.

The sunken vessel is not identifiable from ONI 14, but the closest comparision is Symbol CM-6, OKINOSHIMA class mine layer. The target's gear can undoubtedly be salvaged due to the shallow depth of water in which she was anchored.

- 16 - ENCLOSURE (C)

CONFIDENTIAL

Subject: U.S.S. S-31 - Report of Fifth War Patrol.
- -

CONTACT #7

At 0956(K) on November 1, 1942, a new type gunboat similar to the SHIMUSHU type mine layer was sighted bearing 120° T, distance 3 miles, course 200°T. Went to battle stations, went to normal approach course, and got #3 and #4 torpedo tubes ready which had previously been set at two feet in anticipation of this type target. The sea was glassy smooth with a very slight swell. The sky was cloudless. Before another observation could be made, his screws were heard by the JK to pass astern close aboard at high speed. Course was consequently changed to head for the last bearing of screws. A quick observation showed him on course 325°T with 180° angle on the bow distance about 3000 yards. A few minutes later another periscope exposure showed him changing course to the right to about 090° T and we came to the normal course. Sound could hear nothing. The next exposure showed him bearing 015° relative making high speed on course 050°T at 2000 yards range. Sound picked him up at the same time. Course was changed to follow and sound went out. Due to the sea conditions, I had been exposing about 6" to 1' of periscope for each observation. Because of this, I had not noticed our position particularly although the navigator was keeping a good track. At the last exposure, I saw that the PG had entered the harbor through the usual entrance, distance about 2500 yards angle on the bow 135° port, and that we were practically alongside KURABU ZARI. In fact, in low power I could see the lighthouse base with Japs working there. Right full rudder was applied, the attack was discontinued, and attention was given to getting us out of that entrance without going aground. If I had not been so intent on the attack, I would have recognized the peculiar motion of the ship as we approached shallow water. This fellow was moving around the area too much for us to conduct any sort of a deliberate approach, which probably accounted for the disgusting termination of this contact.

CONTACT #8

This contact is being written up only because of the very unusual circumstances surrounding it.

At 0812 the O.O.D. sighted a large unidentified submarine. The Captain was called to the bridge and upon noting its similarity to our fleet type submarines we dived. The submarine was on a parallel and overtaking course, 0860T, distance about 5 miles (he should have been sighted sooner than he was) bearing 230°T. Crew went to battle stations, #1 and #2 tubes were made ready for firing and course was changed to left to come to the normal approach course to close the range and also get in a position for a straight bow shot. Obtained one glimpse of submarine while

- 17 - ENCLOSURE (C)

CONFIDENTIAL

Subject: U.S.S. S-31 - Report of Fifth War Patrol.

- -

turning; looked very much like CACHALOT. However, the only reference I have to CACHALOT is that both he and I have been notified that there are many friendly ships north of the ALEUTIAN chain. My return track passes through that area, and the only presumption I can make is that the CACHALOT is either ahead of or behind me on the same track. Therefore, I continued the approach in order to identify the strange submarine at least. My next periscope exposure revealed nothing in sight all around the horizon, although by this time the submarine should have been about 4000 yards range. I decided that he dived, so I went to 125 feet in order to avoid any torpedoes should he pick me up by sound. Our sound heard nothing. We had no sooner passed 100 feet than a long series of heavy underwater explosions were heard, sixteen in all. I am not sure they were depth charges, although the sound and sensation are similar. The closest charge seemed to be about 6000 yards away. This new change in affairs seemed to preclude the fact that the submarine was enemy and that our aircraft had sighted and depth charged him. I came to periscope depth to look around and could see no planes or surface ships. However, sea was rough and I could have missed the planes. The question now in my mind was, "should I take a chance on surfacing and get a contact report off, or should I wait until dark conducting a retiring search - patrol during daylight?" The latter course was decided upon because (1) If the fellow was enemy, he very probably was trailing us due to direction finder bearings on my transmissions, which had been plentiful, (2) he could not clear the area any faster than I could and the probability of us both being on similar courses, at not to great a range, was good, and (3) if our aircraft had depth charged him, a report would have gone in immediately.

8. ENEMY A/S MEASURES.
None encountered during contact #1 except that one torpedo may have been fired at us. No coast patrols were observed until the night of 30 - 31 October (K), and then the contacts were 15 and 22 miles from land. We may have missed then because we have been operating within that range, maximum distance from land at night being about 12 miles. No aircraft of any description were noted in the area although a very fine air base is in operation, accordingly to H.O. 255-SA.

9. ENEMY MINE SWEEPING OPERATIONS.
None observed, even though the presence of mine layers indicates mine fields. A notable fact was that ships entering and leaving MUSASHI WAN always passed close to KURABU ZAKI. No mine sweeper was ever observed to be conducting any operations which could be interpreted as mine sweeping. The inference here is that a net or solidly anchored mines may exist along the charted 15 fathom curve to the westward of the observed passage at KURABU ZAKI.

- 18 - ENCLOSURE (C)

CONFIDENTIAL

Subject: U.S.S. S-31 - Report of Fifth War Patrol.

- -

10. MAJOR DEFECTS EXPERIENCED.

1. On October 16, 1942 (Y) when making a battle surface, an apparent misfire which developed in to a hangfire was experienced due to the protective cork plug in the end of the container adhering to the primer in the case of the 4" shell. Upon closing the breech, a small quantity of the cork was compressed into the firing pin receptacle in the breech plug thus preventing the firing pin from making contact with the primer. A leather mallet was used to try to fire the gun by giving the firing pin a sharp rap with no results. The gun was trained abeam and elevated, and the projectile was ejected into the sea. The firing pin receptacle was cleaned out and the next salvo was normal. All 4" ammunition was then inspected and all cork plugs were loosened.

2. On October 22, 1942 (L) during submerged operations, while attempting to pump from regulator tank to sea via the trim manifold, the operator did not throw his 2-way cock in the proper direction which resulted in the trim pump pumping from sea to regulator. In view of the fact that regulator was full the additional pressure placed on the tank before the operators error could be detected, ruptured the bottom of the tank thus making it useless for the rest of the patrol. Reason for failure was corroded bottom of tank.

. On October 27, 1942 (L), the master gyro was out of order for about seven hours while making passage through ONEKOTAN STRAIT. Seas coming down the conning tower hatch, to a depth of one foot on the control room deck, caused water to enter the base of the gyro compass thus shorting out one side of the rectifier circuit. The base was dried out, burned and damaged wiring renewed, all parts wiped down with carbon tetrachloride, necessary parts recoated with insulating varnish (no glyptol available) and a portable heater-blower installed in conjunction with three 100 W lamps. No further trouble has been experienced.

4. On November 1, 1942 (L), the port air compressor became unfit for further use due to the rupturing of the first stage cooling coil. This casualty has become too much of a common occurrence in this vessel and the only remedy is the installation of new coils which DUTCH HARBOR has been unable to furnish.

- 19 - ENCLOSURE (C)

CONFIDENTIAL

Subject: U.S.S. S-31 - Report of Fifth War Patrol.

- -

5. On November 2, 1942 (L), the TAR transmitter would not radiate on high frequency when attempting to transmit by EAST CLUMP. The following day the transmitter was removed from its base and tests were made to find the trouble insofar as was possible with the limited testing equipment aboard. It was found that the high frequency intermediate power amplifier tube and the final amplifier tubes were biased with too much negative voltage on the control grids, thus effectively preventing oscillation and amplification. The bias voltage divider resistor was replaced with no effect. The size of this resistor was reduced by short circuiting a portion of it. This reduced the bias voltage to a value which allowed the tubes to properly operate as amplifiers. In addition, the after "L" antenna was grounded. This ground was repaired and transmissions were then received by CINCPAC - S5 and by NPG - S4. Miller, R. A. RM1c, USN, is credited with placing the transmitter back in commission due to his excellent work and preseverance.

6. At 0130 (L) on November 5, 1942, the Corliss valve operating rod on the starboard C&R air compressor carried away doing minor damage on the casing and valves. This is the second time this casualty has occurred and is due to a bent crankshaft in the air compressor itself. Because of the nature of repairs it was decided to remove the first stage cooling coil from the starboard air compressor and install it in the port air compressor which has been out of commission for some days, (see sub-paragraph 4, this paragraph) due to lack of replacement coil. The port air compressor was in commission by 0600 (L).

7. Upon submergence to 125 feet on 8 November 1942 (Y) with #1 and #2 tubes ready for firing, the after body and gyro pot of the torpedo in #2 tube became flooded although outer doors were closed when passing 100 feet and the pressure vented inboard. The torpedo in #1 tube was found to be normal. The only explanation for this casualty is that the application of takiwax to the exhaust valves of #2 torpedo was not as carefully done as to #1 torpedo and flooding resulted. The torpedo was routined and placed back in service.

8. Number 5 cylinder starboard engine has not been firing since the return trip was started. No opportunity has been found to repair it underway because both engines have been continually in use except during morning and evening dives. The trouble cannot be located under operating conditions but is assumed to be in the fuel pump. Spray air and fuel valve have been cut off. Fuel pump plunger will be renewed upon return to port.

11. RADIO RECEPTION.

Radio reception was entirely satisfactory during the patrol, When in the PARAMUSHIRU area, at about 0300 (K) daily, a great deal of static and interference was experienced, but not enough

- 20-- ENCLOSURE (C)

CONFIDENTIAL

Subject: U.S.S. S-31 - Report of Fifth War Patrol.

- -

to reduce tone quality for reception purposes.

NPM was readable at periscope depth upon several occassions, but NPG was not heard at this depth until our return to the ALEUTIAN AREA.

Transmissions were satisfactory and were very probably made possible by keeping the TAR motor generator dry. No grounds showed up.

On the nights of November 2-3, 1942 (L), the transmitter would not radiate enough to transmit my EAST CLUMP. (see paragraph 10).

Last message received - C.T.G. 8.5 PEACOCK ISLAND.
Last message transmitted - U.S.S. S-31 ICY STRAIT.

12. SOUND CONDITIONS.

The strange underwater supersonic noises, generally known as "YEHUDI", are common to the areas on both sides of PARAMUSHIRU.

All ships observed except two were either anchored, were at a distance greater than 6 miles, or we were on the surface. Therefore the JK did not get a good test. The one sound contact indicated definitely that propeller noises died out at ranges in excess of 2500 yards.

The following data seems to indicate that there are definite temperature gradients both in the SEA of OKHOTSK and the Northwestern Pacific Ocean.

OKHOTSK		PACIFIC	
Depth	Temperature	Depth	Temperature
Surface	49°F	Surface	50°F
45'	48°F	45'	49°F
60'	45°F	60'	47°F
70'	44°F	70'	46°F
90'	39°F	90'	42°F

However, in spite of the comparatively high temperatures as listed above, this observer has recorded temperatures as low as 27°F at 45 feet in both areas in May which may indicate an inversion during that period due to surface ice.

No density layers were encountered.

13. HEALTH AND HABITABILITY.

The officers and crew remained in excellent health throughout

CONFIDENTIAL

Subject: U.S.S. S-31 - Report of Fifth War Patrol.

---

the patrol. Only a few colds were observed. Food was variable and well - cooked. Home made bread was welcomed by all hands.

The boat was very wet on this patrol probably due to the low sea water temperature which was logged between 37°F and 50°.

Morale of the crew was high at all times. There is nothing like hearing torpedoes explode and a good sinking to keep the crew happy.

Casualties:
(1) Ships cook cut his finger in rough seas.
(2) Radioman burned finger making repairs.
(3) Quartermaster suffered face lacerations on bridge in heavy seas.
(4) Lookout suffered possible fracture of rib when seas hit him.

14. MILES ENROUTE TO AND FROM STATION.

Miles to Station	1203 Miles.
Miles on Station	269 "
Miles from TO PARAMUSHIRU	241 "
Miles in PARAMUSHIRU area	951 "
Miles from PARAMUSHIRU to DUTCH HARBOR	1529 "
Total miles steamed	4157 Miles.

15. FUEL EXPENDED.

Fuel used enroute to station	6,714
Fuel used on two stations	9,435
Fuel used enroute from station	10,351
Total fuel used	26,500

16. FACTORS OF ENDURANCE REMAINING.

Torpedoes	Fuel	Provisions (days)	Fresh Water	Personnel(do)
10	2500	10	Full tank	7

17. FACTOR CAUSING END OF PATROL.
Reduction of fuel to reserve limit was the factor causing end of this patrol.

- 22 - ENCLOSURE (C)

CONFIDENTIAL

Subject: U.S.S. S-31 - Report of Fifth War Patrol.

- -

1. Patrol procedure consisted of zigzagging during daylight hours making morning and evening dives to and from station, surface patrol when in area and submerged patrol in areas adjacent to PARAMUSHIRU. Unusually clear and calm weather made daily surface patrols feasible and possible in . When cruising on the surface the battery was floated at 200 amps a side in parallel. When submerged a one motor parallel trim was maintained depending on sea conditions.

A normal one-in-three watch section was carried out by watch officers and crew, while the C.O. and 2nd officer stood a six hour heel and toe duty below decks in order that any possible emergency could be met and handled expeditously. All hands were allowed to sleep except during a short clean-up period daily. The smoking lamp was lighted every two hours during submerged operations, dives on station averaging about twelve and a half hours daily.

2. In view of the recent breakdown of several TAR motor-generators in this type submarine due to excessive moisture collecting in the armature windings, this vessel has had a heating element installed in the end bell of both ends of the M.G. set. This element consists of a 50 W lamp secured to the underside of the inspection plate which is itself raised off the end bell housing by means of extenders secured to the end bell. In addition to the heating element, the M.G. set is run for 15 minutes each watch to insure that no moisture collects on underside of windings.

3. From a reconnaissance of OTOMAYE WAN, it is believed that ships may take departure from this port for the ALEUTIAN AREA. There is a large three storied white building which appears to be an administration center for the settlement. This building is surrounded by smaller unpainted houses. Within a radius of 1/2 mile of this building, there are about 15 warehouses, barracks, two radio stations with 200 foot towers, and several other nondescript dwellings. Also, up and down the coast, two miles from the white building, are located large barracks or warehouses. It is thought that the ship sunk was one which had entered the night before our attack and that the flare or light observed was either a navigational range to guide her in by, or some sort of a recognition signal.

From reconnaissance of KAKUMABETSU WAN and KUJIRA WAN, it is determined that apparently there are no extensive military installations at either place. There is quite a fishing village at KUJIRA WAN, and there are a few warehouse type buildings at KAKUMABETSU WAN. Patrol north of ARAISE ZAKI was not pressed because of the obvious non-military activities of those places already covered on the west coast of PARAMUSHIRU and because there are no other charted anchorages to the northward.

- 23 - ENCLOSURE (C)

CONFIDENTIAL

Subject: U.S.S. S-31 - Report of Fifth War Patrol.

- -

MUSASHI WAN seems to be the location of the "large new naval base" referred to in H.O. 255-SA instead of KAKUMABETSU WAN as stated therein. Installations here are fairly well spread out with a large white building similar to the one at OTOMAYE WAN, several smaller houses, a lighthouse and tower on KURABU ZAKI with several small houses, and a small village at RAISHA. Two AKs a CM and a PG were anchored here during various observations of this bay. Also nine high radio towers are located at the northern end of the settlement. The air field, as shown in H.O. 255-SA seems to be fairly well placed as referred to the hangars. The report, by U.S.S. S-32, that there is a depth of 40 feet two miles off the beach on courses 045°T from Lat. 50-00N and Long. 155-20E seems to be well grounded, and it is thought that this bank has been formed since the 1913 survey by deposits due to the strong flood currents bending around KURABU ZAKI. Every time we approached the 18 fathom curve, the behavior of the ship indicated shallow water.

4. Miscellaneous notes:

(a) It is of little use to approach the island for observation from the west until after 0900 because of the low haze and sun glare before this hour.
(b) Apparently there were but two coast patrol vessels operating when we arrived in these waters, a large one we sank in OTOMAYE WAN; the other was first observed on October 29th(X) in MUSASHI WAN and during the next night he was evidently out looking for us. The last day on station, however, we encountered a gunboat patrolling off MUSASHI WAN. The small patrol vessels are of the light mine laying and gunboat types, and they perform the same jobs for the JAPS that our DMS perform for us in the ALEUTIAN AREA. The small number of naval vessels in these waters would indicate pressure in the SOLOMONS.
(c) PARAMUSHIRU, from my observations of the effectiveness of JAP military bases here, could be taken by a joint operation with carrier based air coverage at this time. There is very little Navy here, no evidence of submarines was observed; no large land batteries of any sort were seen, although it is to be presumed that anti-aircraft protection is good; and the waters seem to be free of mines at present. Good landing sites around the island at strategic points are readily accessible. This statement is merely a personal opinion and may be of no value at this season of the year.
(d) Not a single sampan or fishing vessel was sighted during the nine days spent in these waters. This is the more amazing in view of the fact that fish were abundant and the JK sound gear was frequently interfered with by short range water disturbances attributed to schools of fish.

- 24 - ENCLOSURE (C)

CONFIDENTIAL

Subject: U.S.S. S-31 - Report of Fifth War Patrol.

- -

(e) There are two geographical points named HIGASHI ZAKI. One is on SHIMUSHU TO; the other is on MAKANRU TO.
(f) It is difficult to differentiate between a SHIMUSHU and a NATSUSHIMA type CM at any distance. In view of the uncertainity as to which type is operating in these waters, and in view of the fact that the NATSUSHIMA draws but 5'9" of water, it is suggested that submarines patrolling this area and using MK X-3 torpedoes, keep one torpedo set at two feet during the night, bearing in mind however that the sea must not be too rough in order to capitalize on the shot.
(g) On November 1st (K), a new type patrol vessel was encountered. It is evidently a gunboat carrying 2 or 3 4.7" guns, depth charges astern and looks exactly like the SHIMUSHU type CM except that it has a flush deck. In fact, this PG is surprisingly similar to our PG boats insofar as silhouette is concerned.
(h) It is recommended that all navigational lights be painted over when on war patrol because of the reflecting qualities of the glass covers at night during bright moonlight.

5. It is realized that this report is very voluminous. However, in view of the fact that this submarine is the first one to really have a chance of making any sort of complete reconnaissance of PARAMUSHIRU, all the data obtained and written up is hoped to be of definite value to other submarines going to the same area in the future.

6. The only two actual disappointments of an otherwise interesting and exciting patrol were the failure to intercept an enemy light cruiser force and the unavoidable breaking off of an attack on a coast patrol vessel. Officers and crew did a fine job and the Commanding Officer is gratified by the high standard of patrol efficiency maintained. The diving officer, Lieutenant C.B. CARROLL, USNR, is to be complimented on the excellent manner in which he handled the diving station during the groundings of contact #1.

- 25 - ENCLOSURE (C)

12342
5 0951
1st Copy

FF12-10/A16-3(5)/(16) SUBMARINE FORCE, PACIFIC FLEET

Serial 0543
DECLASSIFIED

Care of Fleet Post Office,
San Francisco, California,
April 27, 1943.

CONSUBPAC PATROL REPORT NO. 172
U.S.S. S-31 - SIXTH WAR PATROL.

From: The Commander Submarine Force, Pacific Fleet.
To : Submarine Force, Pacific Fleet.

Subject: U.S.S. S-31 (SS136) - Report of Sixth War Patrol.

Enclosure: (A) Copy of Subject War Patrol Report.

1. The Sixth War Patrol of the U.S.S. S-31 was carried out enroute to duty in the Southwest, making a seven day patrol around KWAJALEIN ATOLL.

2. Although the S-31 made no contacts during this patrol, excellent reconnaissance was carried out and valuable information regarding the enemy was obtained.

3. The comments of the Commander Task Group Sixteen point Five will be promulgated at a later date.

C. A. LOCKWOOD, Jr.

DISTRIBUTION:
(1M-43)
List III, SS
Special:
F1(5), EN3(5), Z1(5),
Comsublant (2), X3(1),
Comsubsowespac (2),
Subschool, NL (2),
Comtaskfor 72 (2),
Comsubron 50 (2),
Comsopac (2),
Cinclant (2),
Comtaskfor 16 (1).

COMMANDER IN CHIEF
U.S. FLEET
RECEIVED
1943 MAY 13 17 02

E. R. SWINBURNE,
Flag Secretary.

48076 FILMED

CONFIDENTIAL F

Subject: U.S.S. S-31 - Report of Sixth War Patrol.

- -

(a) Prologue:

Moored Submarine Base, Dutch Harbor, Alaska upon return from Fifth War Patrol on November 9, 1942. Departed Dutch Harbor November 12, 1942; Arrived San Diego, California November 24, 1942. Operated with West Coast Sound School between November 27, 1942, and January 3, 1943. Commenced refit period on January 3, 1943. Completed refit on February 8, 1943. Operated with West Coast Sound School between February 8, 1943, and February 21, 1943. Fired seven exercise torpedoes during this period. Departed San Diego, California on February 23, 1943. Arrived Pearl Harbor, T.H., on March 3, 1943. March 8-9, 1943, operated with DesPac Sound School. During refit in San Diego, California, normal work was accomplished, and in addition the following major alterations were completed: (1) Installation of Kleinschmidt Still; (2) SJ Radar; (3) QC-WCA-1 Sound Equipment; (4) ROB broadcast receiver. While at the Submarine Base, Pearl Harbor, T.H., the 4"-50 gun was transferred to the U.S.S. DRUM, and a replacement 3"-50 gun was installed on board. Number 8 fuel oil tank was cleaned and a leak between #7 and #8 fuel oil tanks repaired. Conducted test firing 3" gun on March 9, 1943.

Present Patrol instructions provide for refueling at Johnson Island, seven day station patrol in area, and thereafter reporting to ComSubPac for duty.

(b) Narrative:

11 March, 1943.
1500 (VW) Departed Pearl escorted by PC588.
1730 (VW) Made trim dive.
1900 (VW) Escort dropped 3 depth charges for indoctrinational purposes.
2000 (VW) Released escort. Set clocks to Zone plus 10 time.

12 March 1943.
0615 (W) Made trim dive. Conducted drills.
0800 (W) Sighted PBY parallel course distance 15 mi
0821 (W) Sighted PBY parallel course distance 15 mi
1145 (W) Received NPM 122130 of March.
2100 (X) Set clocks to Zone plus 11 time.
1200 (W) Lat. 19-57N Fuel used 293
Long. 100-44W Miles steamed 171

March 13, 1943.
0535 (X) Made trim dive.
0900 (X) Exchanged recognition signals with B-24.
0958 (X) Made quick dive. Conducted emergency drills.
Made battle surface. Fired ten rounds from deck gun.
Fired all small arms.
1200 (X) Lat. 19-12N Fuel used 1033
Long. 163-56W Miles steamed 188

- 1 - ENCLOSURE (A)

<u>CONFIDENTIAL</u>

F

Subject: U.S.S. S-31 - Report of Sixth War Patrol.

- -

14 March, 1943.

0535 (X)	Made trim dive.		
0914 (X)	Exchanged recognition signals with B-24.		
0930 (X)	Exchanged recognition signals with PBY.		
1008 (X)	Made quick dive. Conducted emergency drills. Made battle surface.		
1200 (X)	Lat. 18-07N	Fuel used	815
	Long. 167-07W	Miles steamed	195

15 March, 1943.

0530 (X)	Commenced zigzagging; approaching JOHNSTON ISLAND.		
0640 (X)	Sighted JOHNSTON ISLAND.		
0645 (X)	Exchanged recognition signals with PBY escort.		
0853 (X)	Anchored in ship channel. Took aboard 2500 gallons diesel oil, fresh stores and cement. (See remarks).		
1440 (X)	Underway for patrol area.		
1200 (X)	Lat. 16-43N	Fuel used	405
	Long. 169-30W	Miles steamed	160

16 March, 1943.

0545 (X)	Made trim dive. Enough water out of forward trim to make complete reload now.		
1200 (X)	Lat. 15-53N	Fuel used	884
	Long. 171-59W	Miles steamed	145

17 March, 1943.

0100 (X)	Set clocks to plus 12 zone time.		
0510 (Y)	Made trim dive.		
1200 (Y)	Lat. 15-05N	Fuel used	876
	Long. 175-20W	Miles steamed	202

18 March, 1943.

0514 (Y)	Made trim dive.		
1812 (Y)	Made trim dive.		
1200 (Y)	Lat. 14-29N	Fuel used	818
	Long. 178-25W	Miles steamed	181

20 March, 1943.

0000 (M)	Set minus 12 zone time.		
0634 (M)	Made trim dive.		
1826 (M)	Made trim dive. Conducted drills.		
2000 (M)	Entered WOTJE five hundred mile circle.		
1200 (M)	Lat. 13-41N	Fuel used	804
	Long. 178-15E	Miles steamed	200

- 2 - ENCLOSURE (A)

CONFIDENTIAL F

Subject: U.S.S. S-31 - Report of Sixth War Patrol.

- -

21 March, 1943.
0537 (M) Made trim dive.
0635 (M) Sighted unidentified plane. Dived.
0712 (M) Surfaced.
1835 (M) Made trim dive.
2310 (M) Made two radar contacts on rain squalls.
1200 (M) Lat. 12-57N Fuel used 1042
Long. 175-16E Miles steamed 180

22 March, 1943.
0550 (M) Made trim dive.
1610 (M) Sighted unidentified plane. Too far away to dive for.
1848 (M) Made trim dive.
1900 (M) Set clocks to minus 11 zone time.
1200 (M) Lat. 12-08N Fuel used 914
Long. 172-03E Miles steamed 197

23 March, 1943.
0510 (L) Submerged. Now 38 miles from area entry point. Has been surprising that we could get this close in without being forced down by aircraft.
1600 (L) Entered area.
1833 (L) Surfaced.
1200 (L) Lat. 11-14N Fuel used 887
Long. 169-16E Miles steamed 170
Present patrol plan is as follows: During daylight hours maintain submerged patrol near ROI and KWAJALEIN ISLANDS and passes; during hours of darkness patrol the rhumb lines between ROI - TRUK, ROI - WOTJE, KWAJALEIN - WOTJE, KWAJALEIN - TRUK while charging batteries on one engine. Due to restriction of only seven days in area, must make the greatest distribution of time for the best coverage.

25 March, 1943.
0508 (L) Submerged, conducting low periscope patrol.
1829 (L) Surfaced. Overcast, no stars, smooth sea, Position doubtful. Patrolling TRUK - ROI ISLANDS rhumb line.
1200 (L) Lat. 09-56N Fuel used 485
Long. 167-58E Miles steamed 111

25 March, 1943.
0501 (L) Submerged. Conducting low periscope patrol. Glassy sea, sky partially overcast.
1248 (L) Sighted ROI ISLAND. Upon closer investigation determined
CONTACT #1 one AK inside lagoon although there may be more.
1320 (L) Patrol vessel headed our way. Spent next hour dodging
CONTACT #2 him.

- 3 - ENCLOSURE (A)

F

CONFIDENTIAL

Subject: U.S.S. S-31 - Report of Sixth War Patrol.

- -

25 March, 1943.

1420 (L) Patrol or escort vessel headed east on about course 090°T indicating he may be proceeding to meet someone in from WOTJE. Will patrol the WOTJE - ROI ISLAND rhumb line tonight.

1833 (L) Surfaced.

2040 (L)
(&)
2100 (L) Radar contacts on rain squalls.

1200 (L) Lat. 09-27N Fuel used 418
Long. 167-22E Miles steamed 96

26 March, 1943.

0505 (L) Submerged. Conducting low periscope patrol. Sighted EDGIGEN Island or DEBUU Island dead ahead. Current set us to south during nite. Set course to close ROI ISLAND.

0814 (L) Sighted three scout type single wing planes circling ROI ISLAND. Also the patrolcraft of yesterday is chugging to and fro.

1843 (L) Surfaced. Commenced night patrol on TRUK - PONAPE - ROI ISLAND rhumb line. Good reconnaisance today verifies one old AK anchored in the lagoon south of ROI ISLAND. There appear to be emplacements on ROI ISLAND.

- 4 - ENCLOSURE (A)

<u>CONFIDENTIAL</u> Jk

Subject: U.S.S. S-31 - Report of Sixth War Patrol.

---

26 March, 1943	in addition to a rather large plane hangar. It is believed that a KISKA type Radar is installed on the N.W. shore of ROI ISLAND
1850 (L)	Radar fix on BIGGESANN ISLAND.
2153 (L)	Searchlight reflection against the overcast from ROI ISLAND, distance 43 miles.
1200 (L)	Lat. 09-28N Fuel used 577 Long. 167-27E Miles steamed 90
27 March, 1943	
0508 (L)	Submerged. Conducting periscope patrol along TRUK - PONAPE - KWAJALEIN ISLAND route.
1500 (L)	Strange squealing and grunting sounds over QC from general direction of reefs, about 10,000 yards range. Undetermined cause.
1850 (L)	Surfaced. Radar fix on KWAJALEIN ISLAND, five miles 046° T. Set course for night patrol along JALUIT - SOUTH PASS route. Intend looking into GEA PASS, SOUTH PASS, and BIGEJ CHAN tomorrow -- there <u>must</u> be some activity [illegible] this atoll.
1200 (L)	Lat. 08-56N Fuel used 550 Long. 167-14E Miles steamed 123
28 March, 1943	
0130 (L)	Bright white light passed overhead, very high - probably shooting star. Point of origin appeared to be NAMU ATOLL.
0230 (L)	Starboard main motor out of commission. Burned out contactor coil #94-A. QC echo ranging gear out of commission. Burned out bearing indicator armature and field.
0513 (L)	Sighted land, later determined to be islands around SOUTH PASS, distance 6 miles. Radar did not pick them up.
0515 (L)	Submerged, conducting periscope patrol. Having difficulty with initial trim and only one motor.
0530 (L)	Sighted dawn patrol taking off from ENNYLABEGAN ISLAND. Under poor lighting conditions, planes appeared to be similar to our old SBU'S.
0620 (L)	Due poor control of boat c/c away from SOUTH PASS. JK picked up patrol vessel's screws.
0730 (L)	Starboard main motor back in commission. Headed back towards GEA PASS.
0820 (L)	Sighted two patrol vessels; picked up their screws. Range about 3000 yards. Changed course to stay outside their sound range if possible. They are typical patrol types.
1020 (L)	Sighted three more patrol type vessels. See description under paragraph (i).

-5- <u>ENCLOSURE (A)</u>

Jk

CONFIDENTIAL

Subject: U.S.S. S-31 - Report of Sixth War Patrol.

- -

28 March, 1943 Sighted two planes, too far away to identify, other
1030 (L) than single wing, circling over ENUBUJ ISLAND.
Trying all day to close KWAJALEIN ISLAND to determine what shipping is inside. Patrol vessels seem to
be very good listeners and every time attempt is
made to get inside them they turn towards us to
investigate. It is suspected that the reason for
so many patrols being out today was due to JAP
radar fix on us when we were in so close this morning
1845 (L) Surfaced. Set course to patrol WOTJE - BIGEJ CHAN
shipping route tonite. Tomorrow intend to get
inside patrol vessel area.
1200 (L) Lat. 08-39N Fuel used 515
Long. 167-41E Miles steamed 105

29 March, 1943 Submerged. Approaching KWAJALEIN ISLAND.
0458 (L)
0729 (L) Sighted two patrol vessels lying to, off KWAJALEIN
ISLAND. Apparently in conference, since no movement for about two hours.
1303 (L) Sighted BOEING type transport over KWAJALEIN.
1510 (L) Sighted a large ship near reef west of KWAJALEIN.
Undetermined whether outside or inside reef.
1530 (L) Battle stations submerged. Commenced approach on
two funnel, three island ship. During approach noted
that target plotted about twenty five hundred yards
inside reef. Decided to fire over reef. Set all
torpedoes at three feet. Continued approach. Determined that high water was due in two hours and that
torpedoes set for three feet would clear the reef.
During approach sighted seven other vessels anchored
in the lagoon. Navigational fix showed us too close
to charted reef for comfort, at which point the
minimum firing range was 5000 yards with 180° track.
No sense in trying to make Mk X-3's run that far
with any reasonable expectancy of success so discontinued the attack.
1835 (L) Secured from battle stations. Set course to clear
area; we are late now due to hopes for successful
approach at sunset.
2028 (L) Surfaced. Clearing area at standard speed. Seven
more days in the area would have produced results;
it is regretted that our patrol on station was of
so short a duration. The only chance of getting
the ships anchored inside is to wait for them to
come out.
1200 (L) Lat. 08-40N Fuel used 329
Long. 167-44E Miles steamed 96

30 March, 1943
0508 (L) Submerged. Conducting high periscope patrol.
1835 (L) Surfaced. Departed area as per operation order.
2100 (L) Transmitted report of contacts to ComSubPac.
Radio Seattle picked it up for us.
1200 (L) Lat. 08-06N, Long. 166-21E Fuel used 465 miles
steamed 92

- 6 -

ENCLOSURE (A)

CONFIDENTIAL Jk

Subject: U.S.S. S-31 - Report of Sixth War Patrol.

- -

31 March, 1943
0515 (L) Made trim dive.
1805 (L) Made trim dive.
1200 (L) Lat. 05-37N Fuel used 922
Long. 165-57E Miles steamed 16

1 April, 1943
0516 (L) Made trim dive.
1818 (L) Made trim dive.
1200 (L) Lat. 02-08N Fuel used 1382
Long. 165-43E Miles steamed 182

2 April, 1943
0350 (L) Crossed Equator. Held appropriate ceremonies.
0512 (L) Made trim dive.
1808 (L) Made trim dive.
1200 (L) Lat. 01-07S Fuel used 1322
Long. 166-10E Miles steamed 140

3 April, 1943
0315 (L) Transmitted NERK 021415
0514 (L) Made trim dive.
1812 (L) Made trim dive.
1200 (L) Lat. 04-45S Fuel used 1295
Long. 167-19E Miles steamed 230

4 April, 1943
0503 (L) Made trim dive.
1745 (L) Made trim dive.
1200 (L) Lat. 08-09S Fuel used 1324
Long. 168-36E Miles steamed 210

5 April, 1943
0517 (L) Made trim dive.
0800 (L) Sighted unidentified plane distance 7 miles on course north.
0802 (L) Submerged.
0823 (L) Surfaced.
1034 (L) ANUDA ISLAND abeam to port distance 6 miles.
1302 (L) PATAKA ISLAND abeam to port distance 23 miles.
1745 (L) Made trim dive.
(L) Transmitted NUBO 051050.
1200 (L) Lat. 11-54S Fuel used 1322
Long. 169-46E Miles steamed 236

6 April, 1943
0510 (L) Made trim dive.

- 7 - ENCLOSURE (A)

CONFIDENTIAL Jk

Subject: U.S.S. S-31 - Report of Sixth War Patrol.

- -

6 April, 1943
0700 (L) Storm making up from south east.
1627 (L) O.O.D. and lookouts sighted object which appeared to be submarine conning tower bearing 090° relative distance 1000 yards apparently on opposite course. Visibility was 1000 yards, heavy rain mountainous seas, wind force 8. Although doubtful if object was submarine, c/c away and remained on surface. Sound heard no suspicious noises. No contact report sent.

2130 (L) Received Subs Seventy Two serial twenty two.
1200 (L) Lat. 15-35S Fuel used 1250
Long. 170-42E Miles steamed 228

7 April, 1943 No diving in this storm; rather ride it out. Wind force 8, sea condition 7, both from S.E., sky overcast, visibility 500 yards to 1000 yards. Position doubtful no sights. Low on both fuel and lub oil.
1630 (L) Obtained fix on FUTUNA ISLAND, indicating a speed of 8.5 instead of 10 knots and a drift of 2 knots setting toward 315°T.
1700 (L) Sighted ANEITYUM ISLAND. Established position. c/c to rendezvous with escort.

8 April, 1943 Wind and sea abating. No trim dive. Supposed to contact escort at 0700(L) but storm has retarted us.
1215 (L) Sighted escort U.S.S. ADROIT, (AM82); exchanged recognition signals.
1200 (L) Lat. 22-08S Fuel used 1370
Long. 169-40E Miles steamed 216

9 April, 1943
1209 (L) Sighted various planes in vicinity NOUMEA. Sighted inbound and outbound ships traffic from NOUMEA.
1300 (L) Commenced steering various courses entering channel.
1526 (L) Moored alongside EDGAR ALLEN POE in NOUMEA HARBOR.
1200 (L) Lat. 22-42S Fuel used 1272
Long. 166-32E Miles steamed 282

- 8 - ENCLOSURE (A)

CONFIDENTIAL   Hn

Subject: U.S.S. S-31 - Report of Sixth War Patrol.

- -

(c). Weather:

From Pearl to the Marshalls, steady northeast trades prevailed with 25% to 50% overcasts most of the time. Full moon all the time in Marshalls. Prevailing winds around KWAJALLIN from east; glassy seas in morning picking up to slight swells and feathered waves during afternoon.

From the Marshalls to New Caledonia, sky was partially overcast most of the time; sea calm. Between Lat. 17S and 20S, encountered winds and seas of gale force from southeast.

(d) Tidal Information:

On rhumb line between Pearl and Johnson Islands it was accurately determined that at this time of the year the current sets 154°T drift .7 knot.

While on north side KWAJALLIN ATOLL, a set toward 180°T of .4 knot was experienced. While on south side KWAJALLIN, a set toward 165°T of .5 knot was found.

Encountered counter equatorial current at 5°N latitude instead of 6°N as expected.

From the Equator to latitude 17°S there was no apparent current although the Pilot Chart showed about .2 to .3 knots to the west. From latitude 17°S to 20°S a storm was encountered which caused a drift of 2.0 knots setting towards 315°T.

(e) Navigational Aids:

No lights at nite encountered in the Marshalls. Chart HO 5428 is not complete. There are islands in the reef line which are not plotted on this chart. Navigational fixes from the plotted islands are fairly accurate.

- 9 -   ENCLOSURE (A)

Hn

CONFIDENTIAL

Subject: U.S.S. S-31 - Report of Sixth War Patrol.

- -

(f) Description of enemy ships sighted:

CONTACT	TYPE	TONS	LOCATION	TIME & DATE
1	FREIGHTER	4000	NO IS. LAGOON	4/25 1248(L)
2	PATROL VESSEL	100	9-26N 167-22 E	4/25 1020(L)
3	PATROL VESSEL	200	8-45N 167-30 E	4/28 0627(L)
4	PATROL VESSEL	200	8-46N 167-31 E	4/28 0827(L)
5	PATROL VESSEL	200	8-41N 167-44 E	4/28 1029(L)
6	PATROL VESSEL	200	8-42N 167-44E	4/28 1030(L)
7	PATROL VESSEL	200	8-40N 157-45 E	4/29 0729(L)
8	PATROL VESSEL	200	OFF KWAJALEIN IS	4/29 0729(L)
9	PATROL VESSEL	200	OFF KWAJALEIN IS	4/29 0729(L)
10	TWO FUNNEL TROOP TRANSPORT	5000	KWAJALEIN IS. LAGOON	4/29 1530(L)
11	TANKER	7000	"	4/29 1530(L)
12	FREIGHTER	5000	"	4/29 1530(L)
13	FREIGHTER	5000	"	4/29 1530(L)
14	FREIGHTER	5000	"	4/29 1530(L)
15	NAVAL AUXILIARY	2000	"	4/29 1530(L)
16	TRAWLER	800	"	4/29 1530(L)
17	PATROL VESSEL	200	"	4/29 1530(L)

Contact number 10 was developed normally but the approach had to be discontinued due to the fact that the target was anchored at too great a firing range on the other side of the atoll reef. The opening range was about 9000 yards and the final range before discontinual of the attack was about 5000 yards. The target was anchored approximately 2500 yards inside the lagoon

- 10 - ENCLOSURE (A).

CONFIDENTIAL Hn

Subject: U.S.S. S-31 - Report of Sixth War Patrol.

- -

(f) Description of enemy ships sighted: (Cont).

and it was considered unwise to proceed any closer than 1000 yards to the reef on the firing course. It is not believed that a Mk 10-3 torpedo has a reasonable chance of hitting at 5000 yards, especially with a small track angle. All other possible targets plotted inside the reef at ranges from 3000 to 4500 yards. Mk 9 torpedoes which has been requested in San Diego were not available there; however, if these had been onboard, it is believed that damage could have been inflicted by firing over the submerged reefs.

(g) Description of aircraft sighted:

CONTACT	NO.	TIME	LAT. & LONG	TYPE	COURSE	ALTITUDE
1	1	MARCH 12: 0800(W)	20-22N 160-12W	PBY	250	1000
2	1	MARCH 12: 0821(W)	20-22N 160-13W	PBY	250	1000
3	1	MARCH 13: 0900(X)	19-20N 163-39W	B-24	250	5000
4	1	0914(X) MARCH 14:	18-15N 166-49W	B-24	250	2000
5	1	MARCH 14: 0930(X)	18-15N 166-50W	PBY	250	2000
6	1	MARCH 15: 0545(X)	15-35N 169-25W	PBY	Circling	1000
7	1	MARCH 21: 0655(L)	13-03N 175-55E	FLYING BOAT	240	3000
8	1	MARCH 22: 1610(L)	11-57N 171-28E	UNIDENTIFIED	160	3000
9	3	MARCH 28: 0810(L)	9-21N 167-27E	SCOUT BOMBERS	Circling	1000
10	2	MARCH 28: 05[illegible]0(L)	8-47N 167-[illegible]7E	"	Taking off	200
11	2	MARCH 28: 0130(L)	8-45N 167-[illegible]7E	UNIDENTIFIED	Circling	1000
12	1	MARCH 29: 1303(L)	8-[illegible]9N 167-44E	TWIN ENGINE TRANSPORT	North	1000
13	1	APRIL 5: 0800(L)	11-24[illegible] 169-41E	PBY	030	1500

(h) Particulars of attacks:

None.

- 11 - ENCLOSURE(A).

fk

CONFIDENTIAL

Subject: U.S.S. S-31 - Report of Sixth War Patrol.

- -

(i) Enemy A/S measures:

Patrol vessel, catcher type, off ROI ISLAND, KWAJALEIN ATOLL.

Patrol vessels, various types, off GEA PASS, SOUTH PASS, and KWAJALEIN ISLAND. Of the five sighted on March 28, two met the description of the "catcher type" from previous patrol reports, two were converted yachts of about 75 tons, and one was a two stack, island, two masted ship, one stack appearing to be false. She was similar to a Hawaiian Inter-Island freighter but on a smaller scale - about 300 tons.

On March 29, it was determined to do our best to get inside the line of patrol vessels around KWAJALEIN. This was done by heading directly for the shore line and then staying as close to the shore as was possible to obtain the required information. It is much harder for the patrol vessel to distinguish our own submerged noises against a shore background than against the open sea background, even though it is granted that the JAPS are good listeners.

The patrol vessels may be very active one day, and the next there will be only two or three, thus indicating that inbound or outbound traffic may be expected. Twice it was observed that after sunset a patrol vessel did not head for the lagoon but disappeared on a course for either WOTJE or JALUIT which might indicate that traffic was expected or that the patrol vessels commute between the various islands.

(j) Major defects experienced:

1. While on the finishing rate, charging batteries on the starboard engine, the starboard motor field suddenly went out. Investigation showed that contactor coil #94-A was burned out, probably from old age. A spare coil was installed and the motor back in commission in 3 hours 30 minutes.

2. At the same time that the starboard main moter failed, it was noted that a hot burning odor was coming from the QC equipment in the control room. The equipment was shut down and subsequent investigation showed that the bearing indicator motor, armature and field, were so badly burned as to be of no further use. No spares were available on board. It is to

- 12 -

ENCLOSURE (A)

CONFIDENTIAL

fk

Subject: U.S.S. S-31 - Report of Sixth War Patrol.

- -

(j) Major defects experienced: (Cont).

be noted that the bearing indicator circuit is the only one in the entire equipment not protected from overload by fuses. The equipment was placed back in operation after short circuiting the bearing indicator elements due to the competent work of Lieutenant (jg) E.I. MALONE, USN.

(k) Remarks:

1. Although it was intended to moor at the fueling dock at JOHNSTON ISLAND, it was determined that an S-type submarine, fully loaded for war patrol, cannot pump up enough to safely clear the twenty foot ship channel. The minimum draft of this vessel under full loading conditions with main ballast (#3 MBT full of fuel) and variable tanks pumped dry, is 20'6" aft; in diving trim 23' aft. Therefore, fueling was conducted from a small barge while that ship was anchored; this worked out quite satisfactorily. Extensive preparations had been made for us to fuel inside the harbor. Fresh fruit, bread, pies, ice cream, and a bottle of beer per man were furnished by the Commanding Officer, N.A.S. JOHNSTON ISLAND, Captain R.W. BOCKIUS, USN., who is to be complimented on the efficient cooperation given us by his station. Thirty two (32) bags of cement were taken aboard at JOHNSTON ISLAND and were deposited in the chain locker in the superstructure forward. This weight, approximately 3000 lbs, was taken on board to compensate for the difference in weight between the 4" 50 gun plus ammunition which was removed in Pearl Harbor and the 3" 50 gun plus ammunition which replaced it. Had this not been done, our last reload would have been incomplete due to the excess amount of water carried in the forward trim tank. The last two torpedoes could not have been loaded without a real danger of broaching due to the light condition forward.

2. Plane sighted at 0635 (M) March 21, appeared to be a KAWANISHI flying boat. Due to the fact that he was 420 miles from WOTJE and ten miles to the south of our track, it seems as though sporadic patrols of the JOHNSTON-PEARL-WOTJE rhumb line may be scheduled to the WOTJE 500 mile circle.

3. The unsuccessful approach on March 29 was most disappointing. All details had been worked out very carefully and it is believed that an attack over such a reef as is located west of KWAJALEIN is feasible and possible with the proper run of torpedo.

- 13 - ENCLOSURE (A)

Rs

CONFIDENTIAL

Subject: U.S.S. S-31 - Report of Sixth War Patrol.

- -

(K) Remarks: (Cont)
Had we been fitted with a few Mk-9's, I have no doubt but that the approach would have produced results. There were no signs of breakers or combers over the reef. Time of high water had been worked out accurately enough to assume a minimum ten foot clearance for a depth setting of three feet. The sea was glassy and a torpedo set for three feet would have run normally. The reason for discontinuing the attack was because we could get into a reasonable firing range on any of the targets without danger of running aground.

4. The following pertinent facts should be of interest to submarine Commanding Officers making future patrols in this area. (a) ENNYLABROAN ISLAND has a landing field from which dawn and dusk air patrols operate. (b) There is an additional island, not shown on the chart, located 1 1/2 miles northeast of ENUBUJ ISLAND. (c) ENUBUJ ISLAND has two large radio towers located in the center of the island with an operating or maintenance shack between them. (d) There are little, if any, indications of a reef between ENUBUJ and KWAJALEIN ISLANDS. (e) KWAJALEIN ISLAND has three definite medium calibre gun emplacements, probably up to eight inch, located on the southwest, southeast and eastern shores of the island. There is also a KISKA-type radar tower located in the center of the island. The radar screen was not observed. (f) There appears to be an air field on KWAJALEIN ISLAND. (g) Ships anchored or moored in the lagoon execute sunset on the SOPA signal of a steady white light at the main. Thereafter, ships signal to one another by means of this all around light. This instance occured twice on successive nights. (h) The coal-burning so-called "catcher" type patrol vessels should always be investigated in order to ascertain that they are not small AK's. (i) The patrol vessel patrol line during daylight appears to be not more than three miles from shore unless a contact is being investigated. No patrols were encountered at night.

5. Submerged radio reception over the loop antenne remained unchanged after NPM shifted frequency from 26.1 KC to 16.8 KC. Rapid fading occurs below 48 feet for S-boats. NPM faded out completely at 1° south latitude 166° east longitude. It was found impossible to transmit our one contact report to NPM; NPC receipted for our traffic.

The SJ radar performed satisfactorily. Ranges up to 40,000 yards were obtained on large islands; up to 13,000 yards on low-lying islands; up to 8000 yards on rain squalls

ENCLOSURE (A)

- 14 -

CONFIDENTIAL Rs

Subject: U.S.S. S-31 - Report of Sixth War Patrol.

- -

(k) Remarks: (Cont)

and up to 2000 yards on water surface. The escort vessel, U.S.S. ADROIT, AM82, was detected at a range of 8000 yards. The receiver was kept tuned on such of these targets as presented themselves. The major portion of material difficulties experienced were tube failures, notably the 6SN7 multivibrators and the 628A thyratron. In addition, the transmitter-receiver exhaust blower shorted out thus blowing the fuses to the filament heater circuits; and the thermo-relay in the exhaust blower circuit opened and stayed open necessitating replacement.

Sound conditions were fair. Propeller sounds from patrol vessels were heard on the JK side of the QC projector at ranges up to 4000 yards. Reefs and land were detected by the increased noise level up to 7000 yards. Fish were particularly noisy on 16 Kc; their whistling being audible at ranges up to 4000 yards.

No density layers were encountered. No echo-ranging was heard.

The maximum consistent depth obtained with the fathometer was 2800 fathoms.

Radio reception was complete.
Last consec. serial rec'd NPM 010937 April ComSubPac ser. 47
Last consec. serial sent NPM C.T.U. 17.2.6 300903 of March.
Last consec. serial rec'd BELLS SUBS SEVENTY TWO SERIAL 31.
Last consec. serial sent BELLS NUBO 090745 of April.

6. The logistic balance for this patrol was estimated to the fraction. We arrived in NOUMEA with 1000 gallons fuel oil on hand and 60 gallons lub oil on hand. One more day's steaming would have been out of the question. The Kleinschmidt still maintained the battery and potable water at a comfortable level.

The morale of the crew remained at a high standard in spite of an unproductive patrol of 4787 miles.

- 15 - ENCLOSURE (A)

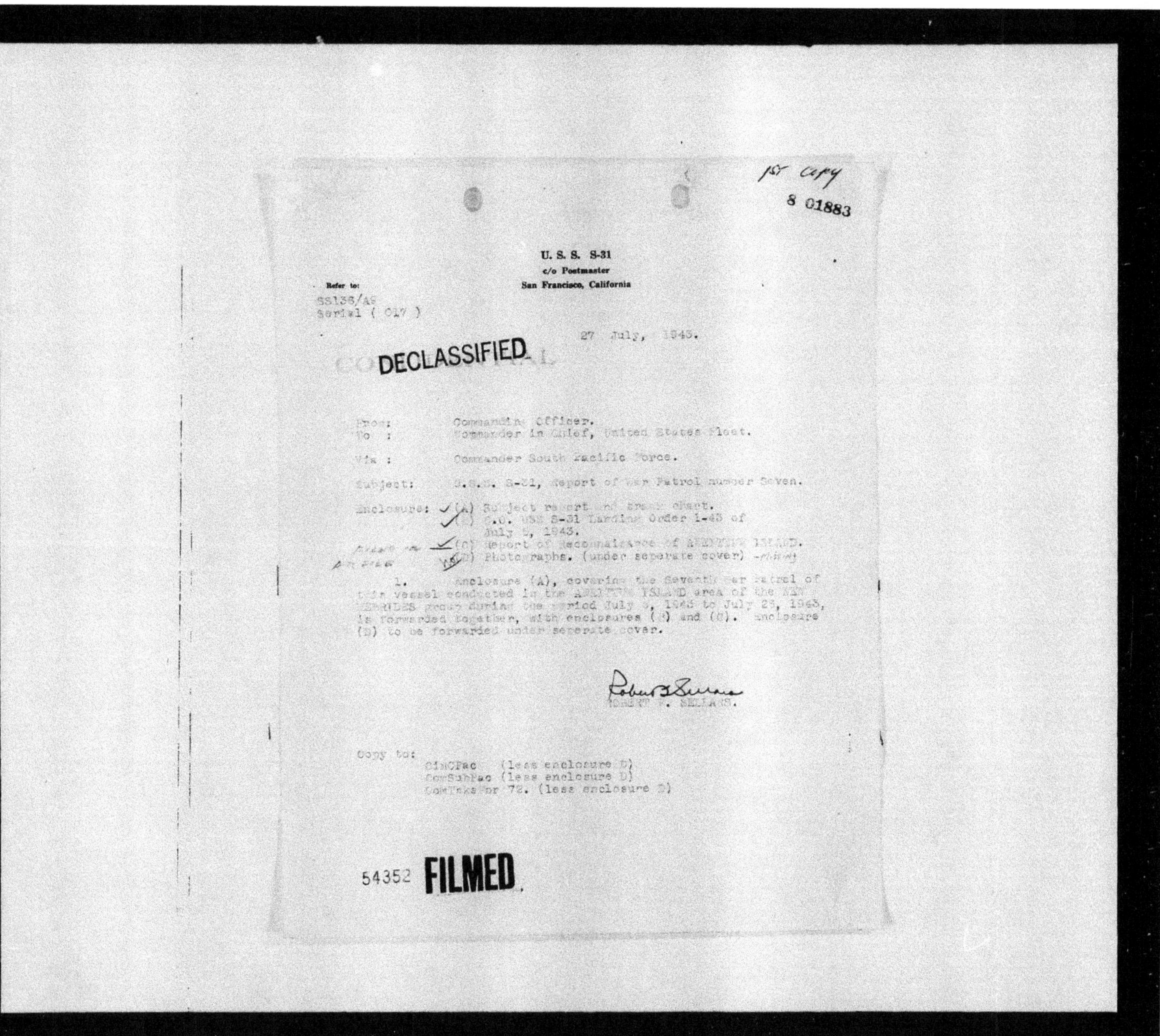

1st copy

8 01883

U. S. S. S-31
c/o Postmaster
San Francisco, California

Refer to:
SS136/A9
Serial (017)

27 July, 1943.

DECLASSIFIED

From: Commanding Officer.
To : Commander in Chief, United States Fleet.

Via : Commander South Pacific Force.

Subject: U.S.S. S-31, Report of War Patrol number Seven.

Enclosure: (A) Subject report and track chart.
(B) C.O. USS S-31 Landing Order 1-43 of July 5, 1943.
(C) Report of Reconnaissance of [illegible] ISLAND.
(D) Photographs. (under seperate cover)

1. Enclosure (A), covering the Seventh War Patrol of this vessel conducted in the [illegible] ISLAND area of the NEW HEBRIDES group during the period July [illegible], 1943 to July 23, 1943, is forwarded together, with enclosures (B) and (C). Enclosure (D) to be forwarded under seperate cover.

ROBERT F. SELLARS.

Copy to:
CinCPac (less enclosure D)
ComSubPac (less enclosure D)
ComTaskFor 72. (less enclosure D)

54352 FILMED

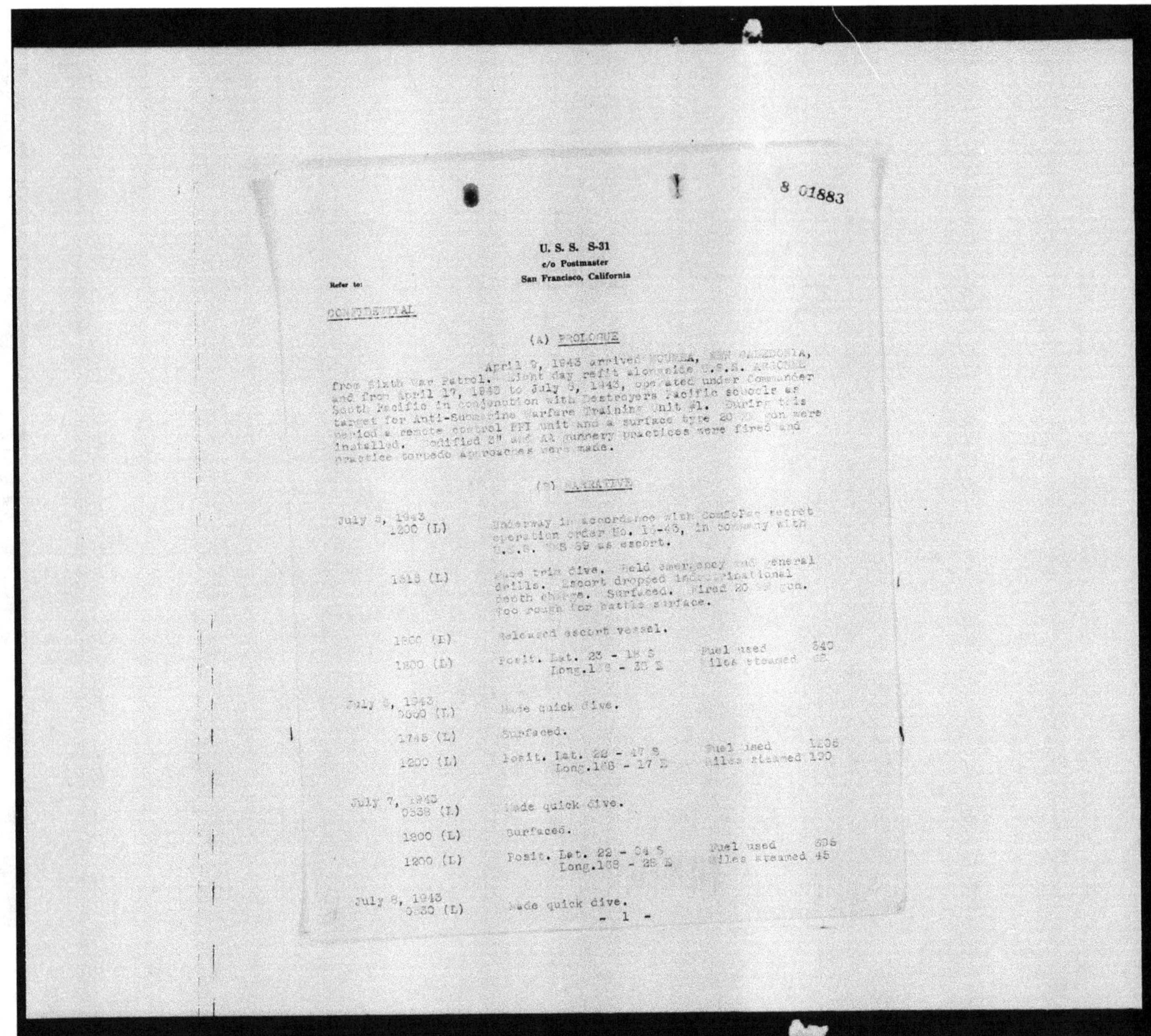

8 01883

U. S. S. S-31
c/o Postmaster
San Francisco, California

Refer to:

CONFIDENTIAL

(A) PROLOGUE

April 9, 1943 arrived NOUMEA, NEW CALEDONIA, from Sixth War Patrol. Eight day refit alongside U.S.S. ARGONNE and from April 17, 1943 to July 5, 1943, operated under Commander South Pacific in conjunction with Destroyers Pacific schools as target for Anti-Submarine Warfare Training Unit #1. During this period a remote control PPI unit and a surface type 20 MM gun were installed. Modified 3" and AA gunnery practices were fired and practice torpedo approaches were made.

(B) NARRATIVE

July 5, 1943 1200 (L)	Underway in accordance with ComSoPac secret operation order No. 1[illegible]-43, in company with U.S.S. [illegible] 39 as escort.	
1515 (L)	Made trim dive. Held emergency and general drills. Escort dropped indoctrinational depth charge. Surfaced. Fired 20 MM gun. Too rough for battle surface.	
1800 (L)	Released escort vessel.	
1800 (L)	Posit. Lat. 23 - 18 S Long.1[illegible] - 35 E	Fuel used 540 Miles steamed [illegible]
July 6, 1943 0500 (L)	Made quick dive.	
1745 (L)	Surfaced.	
1200 (L)	Posit. Lat. 22 - 47 S Long.166 - 17 E	Fuel used 1235 Miles steamed 130
July 7, 1943 0538 (L)	Made quick dive.	
1800 (L)	Surfaced.	
1200 (L)	Posit. Lat. 22 - 04 S Long.168 - 28 E	Fuel used 595 Miles steamed 45
July 8, 1943 0530 (L)	Made quick dive.	

\- 1 -

3 01883

U. S. S. S-31
c/o Postmaster
San Francisco, California

Refer to:

CONFIDENTIAL

(B) NARRATIVE (Cont)

July 8, 1943 (Cont)
0532 (L) — Sighted [illegible] ISLAND dead ahead distance 51 miles.
Made reconnaisance of landing beaches west side of island during day.

1545 (L) — Surfaced. Away landing party composed of: Lieutenant (jg) [illegible] SHAW, USN; [illegible], [illegible](AA), USN; [illegible], PhM1c, USN; and J.G. [illegible], [illegible]2c, USN.

1558 (L) — Made running dive.

1908 (L) — Surfaced.

2100 (L) — Exchanged signals with Lieutenant Shaw via flashing light. At 2400 my message to Captain Downes was cleared by the Army to Efate.

1200 (L) — Posit. Lat. 20 - 20 S, Long. 169 - 53 E. Fuel used 710. Miles steamed 121.

July 9, 1943
0628 (L) — Made quick dive
Reconnaissance northwest quadrant of island.
Took pictures.

1910 (L) — Surfaced.

1918 (L) — Starboard engine out of commission. Cracked #8 cylinder head. See paragraph (K).

2100 (L) — Exchanged signals with Lieutenant Shaw. Zip sub is due to appear in cove, Point "Z", east of Port Patrick tomorrow night. We, and party on the island will be ready for him.

1200 (L) — Posit. Lat. 20 - 20 S, Long. 169 - 41 E. Fuel used 460. Miles steamed 75.

July 10, 1943
0130 (L) — Prearranged signal received from beach indicating NW corner island bears investigation.

0230 (L) — Starboard engine back in commission.

\- 2 -

U. S. S. S-31
c/o Postmaster
San Francisco, California

Refer to:

CONFIDENTIAL

(E) NARRATIVE (Cont)

July 10, 1943 (Cont)

0345 (L) Battle Stations submerged. Approaching northwest quadrant of island on surface; radar gives no indication of Nip sub; shows only usual headlands on beach.

0518 (L) Found nothing near island. Made quick dive. Secured from Battle Stations. Reconnoitered suspected bay. Planned attack for tonite if sub is there.

1812 (L) Surfaced. Patrolling 2 - 3 miles off cove; will intercept enemy when he approaches island since he is not already in cove. No signals from beach tonite; might warn victim away.

1200 (L) Posit. Lat. 20 - 06 S Long. 169 - 48 E Fuel used 380 Miles steamed 63

July 11, 1943

Patrolling northeast quadrant ANEITYUM in close to beach, 2 - 3 miles, in hopes of intercepting expected Nip sub.

0517 (L) Made quick dive.

1808 (L) Surfaced.

2100 (L) Exchanged signals with Lieutenant Shaw on beach. Next expected visit of Nip sub either tonite or 22nd. Patrolling east and northeast coasts of island. Upon return of Lieutenant Shaw with complete information, will send message requesting permission to remain in area until 22nd.

1200 (L) Posit. Lat. 20 - 07 S Long. 169 - 52 E Fuel used 330 Miles steamed 78

July 12, 1943

Nothing in previously inspected coves. Covering east and southeast parts of island. Island obscured by fog.

0545 (L) Made quick dive.

1756 (L) Surfaced.

- 3 -

4

3 01883

U. S. S. S-31
c/o Postmaster
San Francisco, California

Refer to:

CONFIDENTIAL

(B) NARRATIVE (Cont)

July 12, 1943 (Cont)

2130 (L) Closed beach to 3800 yards. Raining. Exchanged signals with Lieutenant Shaw. Natives claim to have seen sub yesterday - me or Nip? Will pick landing party up tomorrow one half hour before sunset.

1200 (L) Posit. Lat. 20 - 15 S Long. 169 - 54 E Fuel used 510 Miles steamed 10[illegible]

July 13, 1943

Circling ANEITYUM from east to north, two to three miles off beach. Heavy rain, visibility 800 - 1000 yards. Radar cuts, with PPI picture, make the problem of navigating in thick weather very simple. It must be remembered that all inspections of bays and coves at night is done by PPI at ranges not exceeding 3000 yds.

0940 (L) Made quick dive.

1300 (L) Commenced approach on beach to pick up landing party.

1638 (L) Surfaced. Landing party returned to ship. Lieutenant Shaw brought back message from Mr. McMillan on TANNA ISLAND that submarine was heard there this morning.

1702 (L) Submerged.

1758 (L) Surfaced. Patrolling a line 2½ - 3 miles off beach, especially watching the north coast of ANEITYUM.

2200 (L) Transmitted NTPO 131015 July to ComSoPac requesting remain on station until 22nd including visit to TANNA.

1200 (L) Posit. Lat. 20 - 03 S Long. 169 - 43 E Fuel used [illegible]30 Miles steamed 93

July 14, 1943

6 Patrolling island on line three miles off beach. Normal patrol line is plotted on chart; circles ANEITYUM 2 - 3 miles from shore. 5

\- 4 -

U. S. S. S-31
c/o Postmaster
San Francisco, California

Refer to:

CONFIDENTIAL

(F) NARRATIVE (Cont)

July 14, 1943 (Cont)

0627 (L) Made quick dive.

1905 (L) Surfaced.

1910 (L) Bright white light on beach. Not signals to us.

1200 (L) Posit. Lat. 20 - 13 S, Long.169-[illegible] E — Fuel used 509, Miles steamed 102

July 15, 1943

Patrolling usual line off ANEITYUM. Starboard engine clutch slipping. Lying to, charging batteries on port engine, repairing starboard clutch, paragraph (E).

0524 (L) Made quick dive. Dive cut short reception of message telling us to remain in area until 22nd. Will get repeat tonite.

1452 (L) Large fire on hillside west coast ANEITYUM. Might be signal to someone else; not to us.

1805 (L) Surfaced.

1850 (L) Lookout stated he saw flare on horizon bearing 270°T. Others say falling star. Keeping sharp lookout - might be answer to fire on hillside.

1910 (L) Small radar pip bearing 290°T changing rapidly to right. Last bearing 000°T showing speed of 152 knots. Probably PBY.

2317 (L) Sighted definite orange flare on horizon bearing 280°T. Secured battery charge, all ahead standard on course 283°T to investigate.

1200 (L) Posit. Lat. 20 - 05 S, Long.169 0 51 E — Fuel used 455, Miles steamed 101

July 16, 1943

0206 (L) Slowed to 2/3 on one engine, charging batteries on other. Nothing sighted; nothing detected on radar or sound gear. Returning to ANEITYUM. Perhaps we were on a wild goose chase while Nip sub made contact at ANEITYUM. Would appear

7 — 6

- 5 -

U. S. S. S-31
c/o Postmaster
San Francisco, California

Refer to:

CONFIDENTIAL

(B) NARRATIVE (Cont)

July 16, 1943 (Cont)

0200 (L) (Cont)	possible in view of conclusions contained in enclosure (C).
0539 (L)	Made quick dive.
0655 (L)	Sighted inter-island steamer on course for [illegible] HARBOR. Similar to "[illegible]" seen in NOUMEA.
0925 (L)	Steamer entered harbor.
1310 (L)	Steamer standing toward TANNA island. Passed 4000 yards astern.
1715 (L)	Surfaced.
1820 (L)	Sighted small fire on shore. Determined not to be signals for us.
1200 (L)	Posit. Lat. 20 - 08 S Long. 169 - 44 E — Fuel used 835, Miles steamed 95

July 17, 1943

0045 (L)	Radar indicates something in cove "B". Island obscured by fog, but PPI guides us in to 3000 yards where it is determined object is part of reef extending into cove.
0130 (L)	Battery charge completed. Making standard speed to get best coverage of island at night. Received ComThirdFlt 132317 of July, granting us permission to remain in area until 23rd. I interpret message as approval to my request to investigate sub report at TANNA ISLAND also.
0531 (L)	Made quick dive.
1805 (L)	Surfaced.
1915 (L)	More trouble with starboard clutch.
2135 (L)	Set course for TANNA ISLAND. Full moon, clear nite. Radar contact TANNA ISLAND at 40,000 yards.

8 — 6 — 7

S 01883

U. S. S. S-31
c/o Postmaster
San Francisco, California

Refer to:

CONFIDENTIAL

(2) NARRATIVE (Cont)

July 17, 1943 (Cont) 1200 (L) — Posit. Lat. 20 - 18 S, Long.169 - 53 E — Fuel used [illegible]50, Miles steamed 117

July 18, 1943 — Conducting PPI search of TANNA coast line for enemy submarines. TANNA has several suitable uninhabited sections of coast for submarine sanctuaries.

0538 (L) — Made quick dive.

1809 (L) — Surfaced. PPI search of coast line.

1922 (L) — Set course for FUTUNA ISLAND will make night PPI search of FUTUNA while returning to ANEITYUM. Enclosure (C) gives reasons for FUTUNA being a likely hideout for Nip subs.

1930 (L) — SJ Radar picked up FUTUNA ISLAND, distance greater than 30,030 yards (off scale).

1200 (L) — Posit. Lat. 19 - 21 S, Long.169 - 25 E — Fuel used [illegible]20, Miles steamed 110

July 19, 1943 0330 (L) — Completed PPI and visual search of FUTUNA. Bright moonlight night. Nothing there, although there are two leeward anchorages which are ideal "stop over" harbors for enemy submarines. Returning to ANEITYUM.

0530 (L) — Made quick dive.

1807 (L) — Surfaced. Patrolling ANEITYUM.

1200 (L) — Posit. Lat. 19 - 53 S, Long.169 - 59 E — Fuel used 450, Miles steamed 87

July 20, 1943 0130 (L) — [illegible] contact in Cove "E". Investigation showed same reef and rock as previously discovered there.

0530 (L) — Made quick dive.

9 — 7 — 8

U. S. S. S-31
c/o Postmaster
Refer to: **San Francisco, California**

CONFIDENTIAL

(B) NARRATIVE (Cont)

July 20, 1943 (Cont)

1812 (L) Surfaced.

1946 (L) Radar contact 7200 yards bearing 188°T. Battle stations. Secured battery charge. Set course 190°T. Ahead on both engines. Visibility 500 yards maximum, slight drizzle. Ready for surface shot.

2002 (L) Radar pip disappeared; had changed bearing very slightly. Presumed to be rain squall. Began zigzagging; slowed down; alert sound watch in case it had been a sub.

2020 (L) All clear; secured from Battle Stations; resumed patrol on patrol line.

1200 (L) Posit. Lat. 20 - 05 S Long.169 - 45 E — Fuel used 510, Miles steamed 99

July 21, 1943

0521 (L) Made quick dive.

1818 (L) Surfaced. Overcast, heavy seas.

1200 (L) Posit. Lat. 20 - 10 S Long.169 - 54 E — Fuel used 680, Miles steamed 112

July 22, 1943

0531 (L) Made quick dive. Weather overcast. Tonite is the night Nip sub should make appearance off ANEITYUM.

1810 (L) Surfaced. Patrolling previously designated line covering the various anchorages in which Nip sub has been reported to charge batteries.

1200 (L) Posit. Lat. 20 - 08 S Long.169 - 54 E — Fuel used 410, Miles steamed 89

July 23, 1943

No ship could have possibly penetrated our search area on the surface tonite. Radar and visual search very complete. Bright clear nite, moon in last quarter.

10 9

- 8 -

8 01883

U. S. S. S-31
c/o Postmaster
San Francisco, California

Refer to:

CONFIDENTIAL

(B) NARRATIVE (Cont)

July 23, 1943 (Cont)

0630 (L) Made quick dive.

1814 (L) Surfaced. Same patrol line as last nite. Intend to leave area about 0300 (L) 24th.

1200 (L) Posit. Lat. 20 - 08 S Long.159 - 41 E Fuel used 330 Miles steamed 98

July 24, 1943

0300 (L) Patrolling north coast AMBITRUM. Clear nite. Departed patrol area. Transmitted NERK 231310 of July to NXZ.

0529 (L) Made quick dive.

1801 (L) Surfaced.

1200 (L) Posit. Lat. 21-09 S Long.166-39 E Fuel used 470 Miles steamed 117

July 25, 1943

0528 (L) Made quick dive.

1803 (L) Surfaced.

1200 (L) Posit Lat. 22 - 48 S Long.168 - 40 E Fuel used 700 Miles steamed 111

July 26, 1943

0440 (L) Contacted large unidentified vessel by radar. Tracked on zigzag course of 285°T speed 13 knots. Going over horizon at dawn.

0715 (L) Contacted escort vessel, U.S.S. SC 725.

1735 (L) Moored to dock at Section Base, Ile Nou.

1200 (L) Posit. Lat. 23 - 02 S Long.166 - 33 E Fuel used 1310 Miles steamed 213

11

10

8 01883

U. S. S. S-31
c/o Postmaster
San Francisco, California

Refer to:

CONFIDENTIAL

(C) WEATHER

There were no unusual weather conditions encountered. Roughly, one half the time was clear, the rest was rainy, and on many occasions the island was completely obscured by a low fog.

(D) TIDAL INFORMATION

(a) The currents encountered between [illegible], NEW CALEDONIA and DURAND REEF are unpredictable, and all suspected reefs should be given a wide berth. The general set and drift is [illegible], one to three knots, variable.

(b) The general set and drift in the vicinity of [illegible] ISLAND is [illegible] - ½ knot. However, between [illegible] and ANIWA ISLANDS, there is a 1.[illegible] knot current setting to the northwest.

(E) NAVIGATIONAL AIDS

The islands of the NEW HEBRIDES group do not seem to be correctly plotted with relation to each other. Attempts to obtain fixes, using the tangents and peaks of TANNA, ANEITYUM, FUTUNA, ANIWA and ERROMANGA ISLANDS indicate that the islands are as much as four (4) miles out of position with respect to each other. However, navigation around each island individually indicates that peaks and tangents are very nearly correctly plotted.

(F) SHIP CONTACTS

No.	Date Time	Lat Long	Type	Initial Range	EST Course Speed	How Contacted	Remarks
1	0855(I) July 16	20-17 S 169-39 E	French [illegible] Island	8000 yds	[illegible] 10	P	Would have made nice shot
2	0440(L) 26 July	20-40 S 167-18 E	Unidentified US, escort	11000 yds	285 13	H	Not sighted

(G) AIRCRAFT CONTACTS

None. Probable [illegible] radar contact on July 16, 1943.

(H) ATTACK DATA

NONE.

(I) MINES

None encountered.

- 10 -

U. S. S. S-31
c/o Postmaster
San Francisco, California

Refer to:

CONFIDENTIAL

(J) ANTI-SUBMARINE MEASURES AND EVASIVE TACTICS

NONE.

(K) MAJOR DEFECTS AND DAMAGE

1. On July 9, 1943, #3 Main Engine cylinder head, starboard, developed a circulating water leak. Inspection showed a two inch crack in the head just below the exhaust valve. The defective head was replaced and the engine was back in commission in four and a half hours.

2. The starboard engine clutch has been an intermittent casualty for sometime. The shoes wear so rapidly that it necessitates putting an engine and motor out of commission about every other week to adjust the clutch. The shoes were new in June; they are now so worn that replacement is necessary. This condition is caused by a worn main motor thrust bearing which allows the motor and stub shaft to slide fore and aft with about one eighth inch movement. Defect will be remedied during the coming overhaul of this vessel.

(L) RADIO

Radio performance was satisfactory at all times. NPM, on 16.[illegible] kcs, was copied, as a test, down to 59 feet. This was done in order to note any effective difference in submerged loop reception due to change in height of loop antenna.

First serial received	NL 605 of July 5, 1943.
Last serial received	NL 833 of July 28, 1943.
First despatch sent	NERO 131015 of July.
Last despatch sent	NERO 281310 of July.

(M) RADAR

Radar performance was excellent at all times. The usual number of tube failures was experienced, and, at one time, it was noticed that objects between 180° and 230° relative gave extremely erratic pips. To remedy this defect the feeder unit tuning plunger assembly was removed and cleaned. A considerable amount of dust was blown out of the wave guide, the assembly replaced, and the trouble disappeared. Later, a range of about 70,000 yards was obtained on a 2,000 foot island. At another time, the indicator trace to the left of the range step became erratic. This trouble was traced to condenser C-47 in the Range Unit.

- 11 -

8 01883

U. S. S. S-31
c/o Postmaster
San Francisco, California

Refer to:

CONFIDENTIAL

(M) RADAR (Cont)

The Plan Position Indicator, installed last month, gave generally excellent results. It proved invaluable for navigation in restricted waters during reduced visibility. It proved a fool-proof means of searching the shore line in any kind of weather, which aided our particular mission greatly. Reefs, 200 - 300 yards from the beach, were detected at ranges up to 10,000 yards. With a pencil sketch of the island in hand, the radar operators had no trouble locating and recognizing the exact points upon which the CO wanted ranges and bearings taken. All submarines should be equipped with a remote control PPI unit for purposes of tracking the enemy as well as for navigational uses.

(N) SOUND GEAR AND SOUND CONDITIONS

The [illegible]-1 sound gear was running continuously during the entire patrol. Results were satisfactory; there were no failures. The fathometer was used sparingly, and then only when it was suspected that water depths were embarrassingly shallow.

Sound conditions in the [illegible] area were excellent. The only ship contact was followed out to 10,000 yards at which range the propeller beats still came in intermittently.

(O) DENSITY LAYERS

During this patrol, a surface ship bathythermograph was borrowed from Anti-Submarine Warfare Training Unit #1 and altered to fit into the submerged signal ejector. By this means, several readings were taken to depths of 150 feet, no necessity being found to go deeper. The glass plates showed practically a straight line, thus indicating no thermal or density layers in the vicinity of [illegible] ISLAND at this time. A permanently installed bathythermograph will be installed during the forth coming overhaul.

(P) HEALTH, FOOD, AND HABITABILITY

The health of officers and crew was excellent; the food was normal and well balanced; and the habitability was not uncomfortable for an S-type submarine.

(Q) PERSONNEL

The performance of duty of officers and men, under the more or less tiresome conditions of a "watch-and-wait" patrol, was gratifying. Morale of personnel is now higher than it has been

\- 12 -

R 01883

U. S. S. S-31
c/o Postmaster
Refer to: **San Francisco, California**

CONFIDENTIAL

(Q) PERSONNEL (Cont)

since this vessel commenced operations with Anti-Submarine Warfare Training Unit #1 in April.

(R) MILES STEAMED - FUEL USED

Base to Area	331 miles	2260 gallons
In Area	1567 miles	8170 gallons
Area to Base	378 miles	2520 gallons

(S) DURATION

Days enroute to area	3
Days in area	16
Days enroute to base	3
Days submerged	20

(T) FACTORS OF ENDURANCE REMAINING

TORPEDOES	FUEL	PROVISIONS	PERSONNEL FACTOR
12	14,970	15	15

Limiting factor this patrol: Orders Commander South Pacific.

(U) REMARKS

1. Lieutenant (jg) W.R. SHAW, USN., is to be complimented on the manner in which he handled all details of the landing party put on AN[illegible]TYUM ISLAND for the purpose of establishing a system of signals to let this vessel know of the presence of an enemy submarine in the vicinity. His report is appended as enclosure (C).

2. It is believed that in view of U.S. operations in the SOLOMON ISLAND area at present, all Nip submarines were recalled to that area, thus accounting for the fact that no further enemy submarine contacts were made by the island watchers during the time this vessel was in the ANEITYUM vicinity. A close and accurate watch was kept on the island at all times except for two days when the

15 14

- 13 -

S 31883

U. S. S. S-31
c/o Postmaster
Refer to: **San Francisco, California**

CONFIDENTIAL

(U) REMARKS (Cont)

islands of TANNA and FUTUNA were searched.

3. By the process of elimination, it appears that the primary reason for any Jap subs being in this area is for a low frequency low power communication relay system, and secondly for what information they could pick up among the natives. It is strongly suggested that SALLY, referred to in Enclosure (C), be watched and investigated.

4. The suggestion, contained under Conclusions in Enclosure (C), concerning the use of small submarines as "behind-the-line investigators" is concurred in except that such submarines, when available, should have the primary mission of hunting down Jap reconnaissance subs and destroying them.

16 15

22807

8 01883

COMSOPAC FILE
A16-3/(11)

Serial 01355

SOUTH PACIFIC FORCE
OF THE UNITED STATES PACIFIC FLEET
HEADQUARTERS OF THE COMMANDER

bco

C-O-N-F-I-D-E-N-T-I-A-L

14 AUG 1943

1st Endorsement on
CO USS S-31 Conf. ltr.
SS136/A9, Serial 017,
dated July 27, 1943.

From: The Commander South Pacific.
To : The Commander-in-Chief, United States Fleet.

Subject: USS S-31 (SS 136) - Report of Seventh War Patrol, Comments on.

1. Forwarded.

2. The repeated reports from natives and white citizens of Aneityum Island point most conclusively to the fact that Japanese submarines are using this area for re-charging batteries. The logic and reason for accomplishing this so close to an occupied island is not known.

3. The report of performance of Plan Position Indicator suggests it would be a most valuable item of equipment for all submarines.

4. The Commander South Pacific congratulates the Commanding Officer, officers and crew of the S-31 on a thorough and energetic patrol. It is regretted that no contacts with enemy were made. For purposes of award of the submarine combat insignia however, this cannot be classed as a successful patrol.

W. F. Halsey

W. F. Halsey

1943 AUG 24 16 42
COMMANDER IN CHIEF
U.S. FLEET
RECEIVED

Copy to:
CincPac
ComSubPac
ComTaskFor 72
CO USS S-31

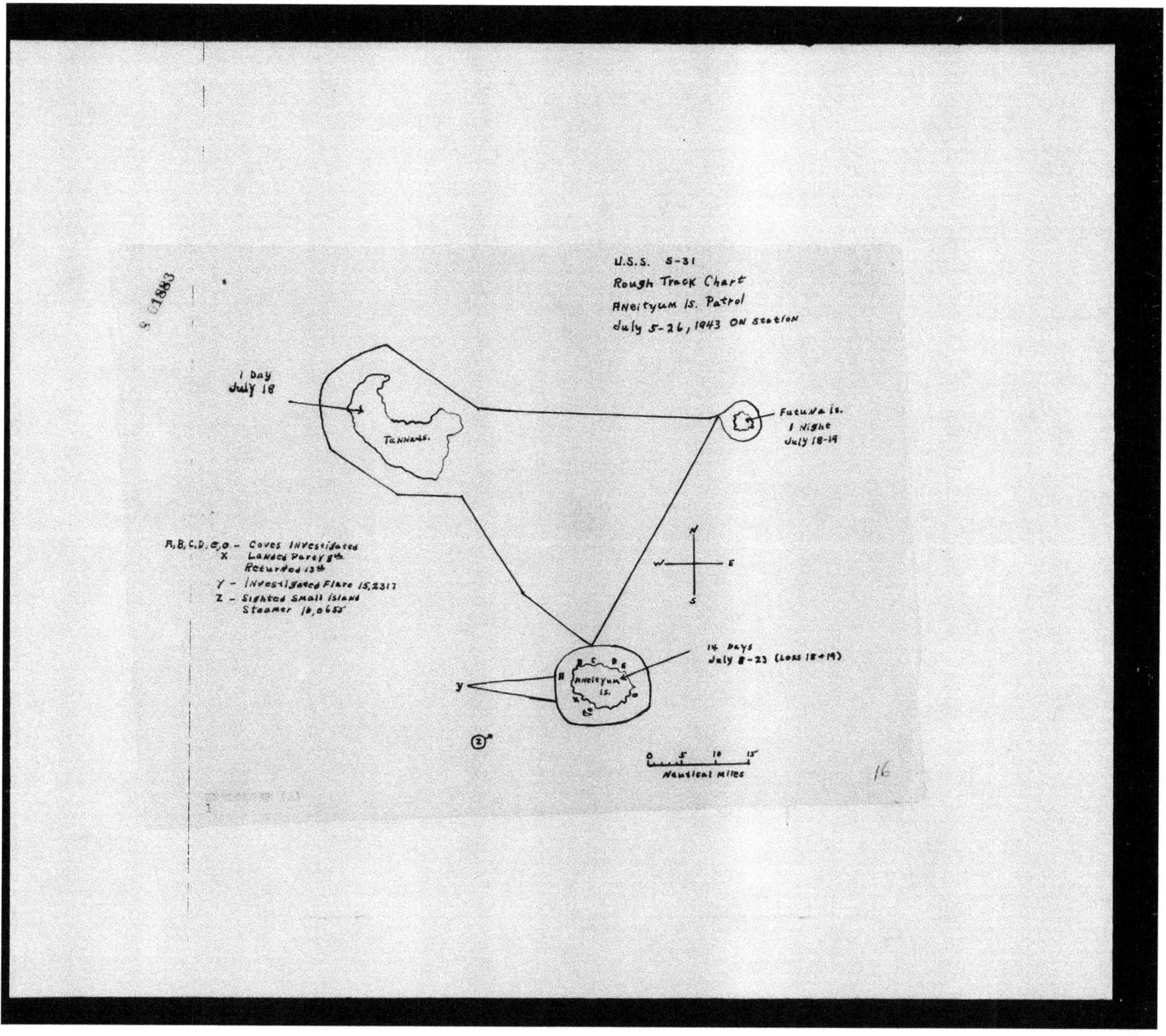
U.S.S. S-31
Rough Track Chart
Aneityum Is. Patrol
July 5-26, 1943 On station
1 Day
July 18
Tanna Is.
Futuna Is.
1 Night
July 18-19
A, B, C, D, E, O - Coves Investigated
X Landed Party 9th
Returned 13th
Y - Investigated Flare 15, 2317
Z - Sighted Small Island
Steamer 16, 0655
N
W
E
S
14 Days
July 8-23 (Less 18+19)
Aneityum Is.
y
0 5 10 15
Nautical Miles

S 61883

U. S. S. S-31
c/o Postmaster
San Francisco, California

Refer to:

SS136/A16-3

July 6, 1943.

C-O-N-F-I-D-E-N-T-I-A-L

LANDING ORDER #1-43

Objective is to establish a means of interchanging signals between U.S. Army watchers on ANEITYUM ISLAND and U.S.S. S-31 to let this vessel know when and where an enemy submarine is sighted in the vicinity.

At twilight or dawn, depending on the tactical situation, S-31 will land one rubber boat, at a predetermined spot, manned by one officer and 3 men, properly equipped, to stay ashore for a period as long as 3 days. This party will contact the Army coast watchers and make the necessary arrangements as to signals. It is understood that the watchers speak French only. Party will probably be landed one day and taken off the next; this provision is subject to change by message.

It is not definitely known if the enemy is on the island. All necessary precautions will be taken to ensure the greatest safety to personnel. The O in C of landing party will be responsible for making all necessary communication and recognition arrangements with island watchers.

Communications by hooded blinker flashlights at night. During daylight, in order to indicate which quadrant of island bears investigation, smoking fires will be used as follows: South West - one; Northwest - two; Northeast - three; Southeast- four. At night flashlight signals as follows: South West - one dot; Northwest - two dots; Northeast - three dots; Southeast - four dots. All signals to be consecutively repeated 3 times followed by the letter designation of suspected enemy submarine location. Other or amplifying communications by International Code. Coves designated as follows, starting with ANEITYUM HARBOR clockwise; Cove X, next probable A; next B; C; D; E; and C as previously designated.

If an alternate landing point is required Point C, just South of [illegible] Point, in quadrant four, is designated. Other conditions remain unchanged.

18 17

\- 1 -

ENCLOSURE (B)

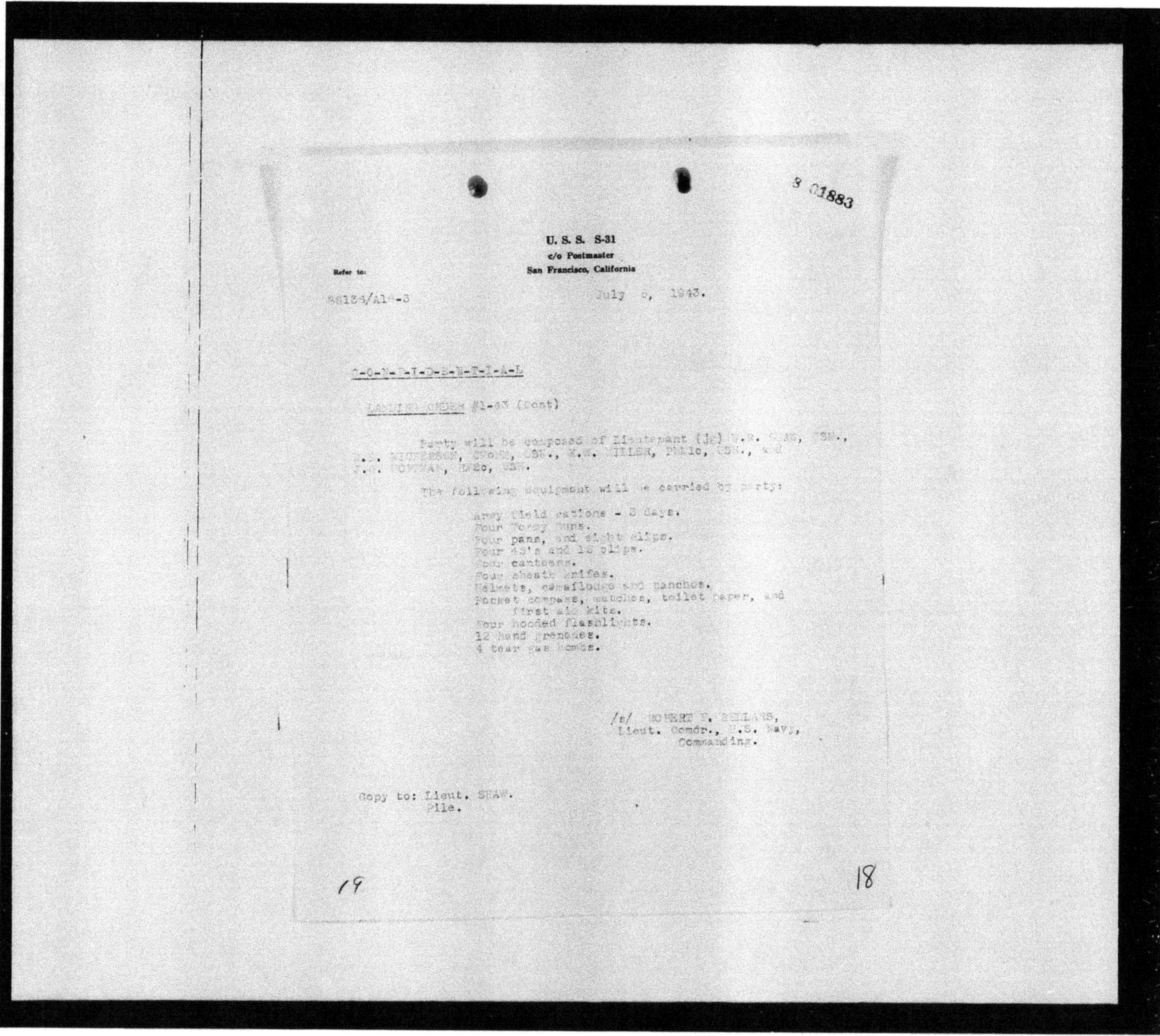

3 01883

U. S. S. S-31
c/o Postmaster
San Francisco, California

Refer to:

SS133/A16-3

July 6, 1943.

C-O-N-F-I-D-E-N-T-I-A-L

LANDING ORDER #1-43 (Cont)

Party will be composed of Lieutenant (jg) [illegible] SHAW, USN., [illegible], [illegible], USN., K.N. MILLER, PhM1c, USN., and J.[illegible] [illegible], [illegible]2c, USN.

The following equipment will be carried by party:

Army field rations - 3 days.
Four Tommy Guns.
Four pans, and eight clips.
Four 45's and 12 clips.
Four canteens.
Four sheath knifes.
Helmets, camaflodge and panchos.
Pocket compass, matches, toilet paper, and
first aid kits.
Four hooded flashlights.
12 hand grenades.
4 tear gas bombs.

/s/ ROBERT F. SELLARS,
Lieut. Comdr., U.S. Navy,
Commanding.

Copy to: Lieut. SHAW.
File.

19

18

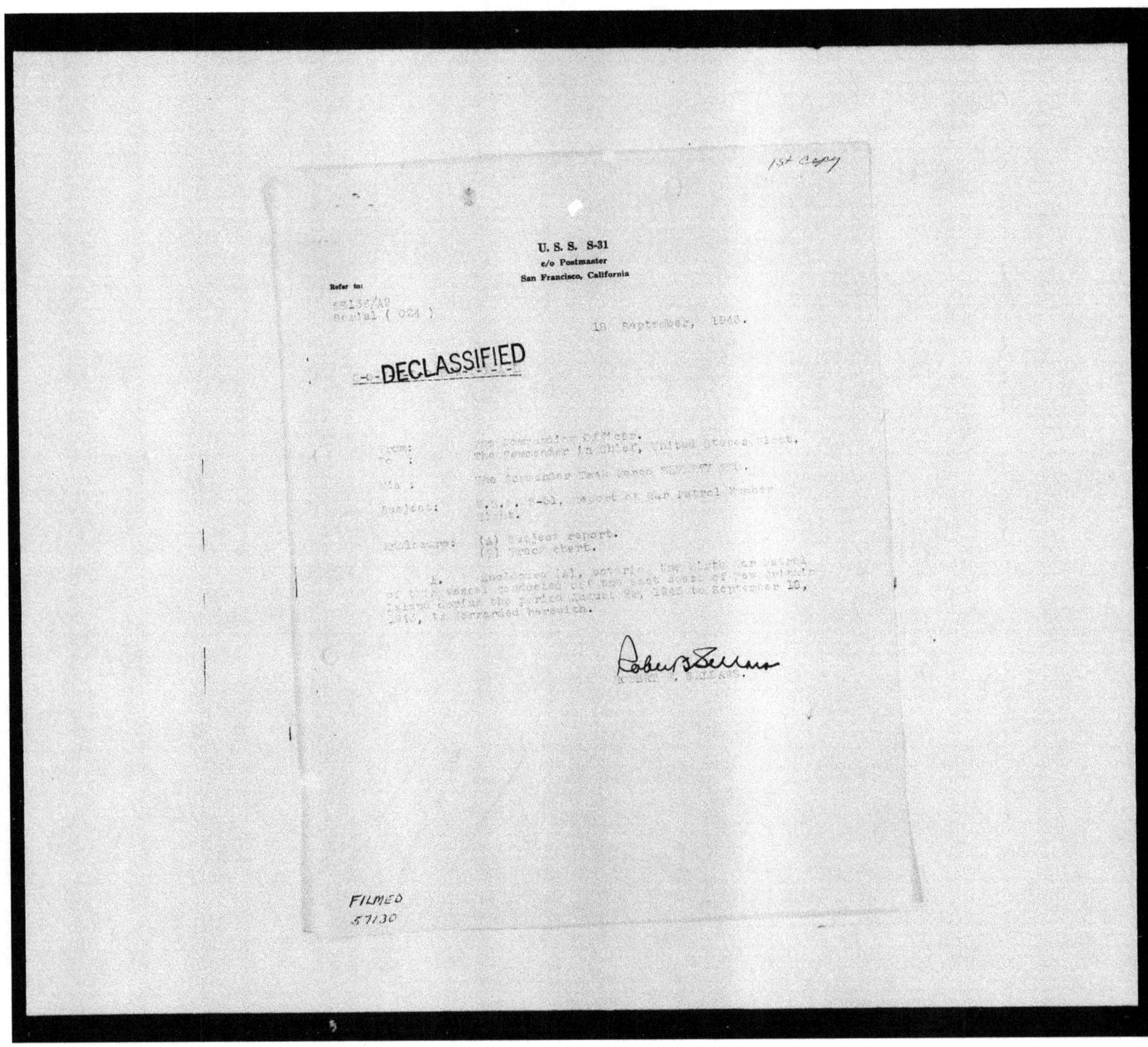

1st Copy

U. S. S. S-31
c/o Postmaster
San Francisco, California

Refer to:
SS136/A9
Serial (024)

19 September, 1943.

DECLASSIFIED

From: [illegible]
To : The Commander in Chief, United States [illegible].
Via : The Commander Task Force [illegible].
Subject: [illegible] S-31, Report of War Patrol Number [illegible].
Enclosures: (A) Subject report.
(B) Track chart.

1. Enclosure (A), [illegible] of this vessel conducted [illegible] during the period [illegible] 1943 to September 10, 1943, is forwarded herewith.

[illegible]

FILMED
57130

CONFIDENTIAL

(A) PROLOGUE

Returned from Seventh War Patrol on July 26, 1943 and resumed duties with Anti-Submarine Warfare Training Unit Number One; conducted operations in the NOUMEA - HAVANNAH HARBOR area until August 20, 1943. August 12, 1943 executive officer detached; August 19, 1943 third and fourth officers detached. August 21, 1943 one day upkeep; departed on Eighth War Patrol on August 22, 1943. Officers on board:

Lieut-Comdr., ROBERT F. SELLARS, USN.
Lieut. (jg) E.I. Malone, USN.
Lieut. (jg) W.R. Shaw, USN.
Ensign S.N. Donahoe, USNR.

(B) NARRATIVE

Sunday, August 22, 1943

1400 (L) Underway for patrol area in accordance with CTF-72 operation order S48-43, as task unit 72.1.2. Escort U.S.S. PC 1267.

1700 (L) Made trim dive.

1830 (L) Released escort vessel.

Monday, August 23, 1943.

0542 (L) Made morning dive. Heavy weather. Surfaced, commenced zigzagging. Holding fire control drills daily.

1745 (L) Made evening dive. Surfaced, ceased zigzagging.
1200 (L) Lat 16-26 S FUEL USED 930
Long 165-31 E MILES STEAMED 154

Tuesday, August 24, 1943.

Received more dope about Nip sub habits off ORFORD from CTF-72. No dive this AM; charging batteries. Heavy seas from S.E. Visibility 5 miles. Pooping seas have practically drowned out the control room.

1200 (L) Changed speed to standard. Sun lines show us behind schedule. No evening dive; overcast squally weather, visibility 2 miles.
1200 (L) Lat 15-40 S FUEL USED 1040
Long 163-00 E MILES STEAMED 152

- 1 -

CONFIDENTIAL (B) NARRATIVE (Cont)

Wednesday, August 25, 1943:
0555 (L) Made morning dive. Still overcast, seas rough. Surfaced. Eliminated small oil leak which had been causing slick. Also found reserve lub oil tank emulsified with slight salty taste. This will mean more work for the enigineers as regards running purifier. Remaining on surface today in order to catch up to schedule. Encountered heavy tropical storm, wind 50 m.p.h. during afternoon.

1810 (L) Made evening dive. Surfaced.
1200 (L) Lat 14-00 S FUEL USED 460
Long 160-00 E MILES STEAMED 158

Thursday, August 26, 1943.
0555 (L) Made quick dive. Conducting submerged patrol at periscope depth. Weather overcast for last four days. Surfaced. Nothing sighted during the day. Have been holding drills, emergency and fire control, daily; but now on it's the real thing.

1600 (L) Port C&R air compressor out of commission. (See paragraph ("K").
1200 (L) Lat 12-00 S FUEL USED 890
Long 158-15 E MILES STEAMED 158

Friday, August 27, 1943.
During the period 2300(L)/26 to 0430(L)/27, radio reported a definite key clicking noise on the 800 Kc's band which they could not tune in at any time. It sounded close.

0100 (L) Set clocks to Zone - 10 time.

0510 (K) Made quick dive. Maintaining periscope patrol.

0630 (K) Lost power to both main motors. Held depth at 38 feet. (See paragraph "K").

0715 (K) Power to starboard main motor; going ahead. Port main motor contactor coil burned out; will have repaired in six hours. Due to poor depth control with one motor parallel - parallel trim, remained at 60 feet until port motor contactor coil replaced.

- 2 -

6 4

CONFIDENTIAL (B) NARRATIVE(cont)

Friday, August 27, 1943 (Cont)

1720 (K) Port main motor contactor panel repaired, going ahead both motors, normal parallel.

1818 (K) Surfaced.
1200 (K) Lat 10-44 S FUEL USED 640
Long 156-37 E MILES STEAMED 122

Saturday, August 28, 1943.

Received more dope on subs passing ORFORD.

0500 (K) Made quick dive. Conducting periscope patrol.

1822 (K) Surfaced.
Find from despatches that we will have four blue subs, two Nip DF's and another blue sub to contend with today. From available information, we shouldn't bother the GREENLING, but we should pass between #1 and #2 of the group of four about noon today, working on the presumption that they are spaced about 60 miles.
1200 (K) Lat 9-24 S FUEL USED 520
Long 155-23 E MILES STEAMED 108

Sunday, August 29, 1943.

Another Nip sub off ORFORD today.

0515 (K) Made quick dive. Periscope patrol. It appears that, from an analysis of the times of contact of the various Nip subs off ORFORD, that the average speed of the southbound subs is about 10 - 12 knots if they leave RABAUL at daylight. Conversely, the speed of the northbound subs must be about 12 - 15 knots if they leave LAE or SALMAUA at a reasonable time in the morning.

1827 (K) Surfaced.
1200 (K) Lat 08-01 S FUEL USED 550
Long 154-02 E MILES STEAMED 117

- 3 -

CONFIDENTIAL (B) NARRATIVE (Cont'd)

Monday, August 30, 1943.
There has been at least one sub sighted daily off CAPE ORFORD, since the 23rd.

0507 (K) Made quick dive. Conducting periscope patrol.

1830 (K) Surfaced.

2012 (K) Radar contact NEW BRITAIN, land at 60,000 yards.
1200 (K) Lat 6-31 S FUEL USED 560
Long 152-45 E MILES STEAMED 113

Tuesday, August 31, 1943.
0280 (K) Entered area off CAPE ORFORD. Am placing myself to intercept morning northbound sub. The following is a brief resume' of Nip sub. sightings recently off CAPE ORFORD:

SOUTHBOUND	NORTHBOUND
8/18/1400	8/17/0856
8/22/1600	8/20/0930
8/24/1440	8/24/0900
8/27/1430	8/26/0630
8/28/1500	8/28/0845

From this schedule, it shouldn't be hard to eliminate one of them.

0505 (K) Made quick dive. Patrolling on course 015°T - 195°T. Weather squally, with occasional clearings.

0941 (K) Sound picked up propeller noises. Periscope observation showed rain.

0943 (K) Periscope observation showed Nip submarine of I-52 class emerging from squall. Battle stations submerged, swung to normal approach course. Initial range 5000 yds., 90° starboard track. Came to normal approach course, increased speed to 2500 amps a side, and tried to close him. Upon getting tubes ready for firing the torpedoman left the forward trim valve partially open thus flooding forward trim tank through the tubes. We levelled off at 130 feet before trim was regained. In the meantime the

- 4 -

6 6

CONFIDENTIAL (D) NARRATIVE (Cont'd)

Tuesday, August 31, 1943.

the targets propeller noises were becoming fainter and the bearing crossed the bow. Closest range estimated at 4500 yards on about a 125° starboard track.

1015 (K) Target faded out. Secured from Battle Stations.

1422 (K) Sound picked up propeller sounds. Periscope observation showed Nip sub of I-61 class heading our way. Battle Stations submerged. Next periscope observation showed engine exhaust smoke, but no submarine. Resting easy on battle stations, tubes ready, until sound picked up target, which had evidently dived.

1504 (K) Submarine surfaced, dead astern, range 1200 yards, making me wish we had stern tubes. Commenced swinging for bow shot.

1507 (K) Fired three (3) torpedoes. No hits.

1512 (K) Two fairly close aerial depth charges. Rigged for depth charge attack, and commenced evasive tactics at seventy feet. Periscope look showed target zigzagging radically to south. No plane in sight.

1553 (K) Secured from depth charge attack and Battle Stations.

1940 (K) Surfaced, Heading south to clear ORFORD for one day. We were undoubtedly sighted after firing since the periscope was up at 6 knots, speed caused an appreciable slick astern, and impulse bubbles could plainly be seen in this water. The impulse bubble slicks were evidently the point of aim for the aerial depth charges.

2200 (K) Received news that two subs were seen off ORFORD again today. Most embarrassing to me; in fact, this was probably my most disappointing day in submarines.

1200 (K)	Lat 5-27 S	FUEL USED	590
	Long 152-12 E	MILES STEAMED	105

Wednesday, September 1, 1943.

0527 (K) Made quick dive. We are now thirty miles south of CAPE ORFORD, attempting to cover the dawn positions of northbound Nip sub. Will work towards ORFORD during the day. The Nips have undoubtedly

- 5 -

9 7

Wednesday, September 1, 1943. (Cont'd)

changed their sub schedule or their routing by now.

1832 (K)Surfaced. No contacts during day.

2200 (K)Received word of Nip sub sighted ten miles east of ORFORD today. Will head out to cover that line tomorrow.

2210 (K)Received word of a cruiser, and AK and a Nip sub in WIDE BAY. Immediately heading for WIDE BAY; deep water all the way in; can take a look and still get out to patrol line to intercept Nip sub at noon tomorrow.

1200 (K)	Lat 5-55 S	FUEL USED	490
	Long 151-39 E	MILES STEAMED	75

Thursday, September 2, 1943.

Weather overcast, constant lighting, intermittent squalls, visibility zero. Covering entrances to WIDE BAY in case Nips stand out during nite. Several lights noticed moving around on beach in vicinity CRATER POINT.

0500 (K)Reversed course in order to arrive at Nip sub interception point by noon.

0515 (K)Made quick dive.

1831 (K)Surfaced.

2000 (K)Received news of another northbound Nip sub at noon today. This is becoming definitely embarrassing, since at noon today we were ten miles off CAPE ORFORD,,conducting a high periscope patrol, taking a look every fifteen minutes. How he got by without going aground at ORFORD is a miracle. Tomorrow plan to patrol a four mile square two miles off CAPE ORFORD and see if anyone can get by.

1200 (K)	Lat 5-29 S	FUEL USED	370
	Long 152-14 E	MILES STEAMED	86

Friday, September 3, 1943.

Sighted lights moving near CRATER POINT and near village between CRATER POINT and CAPE ORFORD. Very clear night, sea smooth, visibility good.

- 6 -

10 8

Friday, September 3, 1943 (Cont'd).

0312(K) O.O.D. sighted flare which looked to be a search-light close aboard. Made quick dive. C.O. then identified flares through periscope.

0325(K) Surfaced. The flares, if they were 200 feet altitude, could be seen for 21 miles, and on the bearing taken, would show them in the vicinity of JAMMER BAY on the north coast of WIDE BAY.

0500(K) Made quick dive. Patrolling on a line bearing 115°T from CAPE ORFORD, 2 to 6 miles off. If a sub gets by us today, it will be because he passed at least 12 miles off the CAPE.

1849(K) Surfaced. Glassy sea, bright sun all day. Noted that at periscope depth the 3" gun bright work makes us a fine target. Will remedy that tonite.

2030(K) Noted searchlight display from RABAUL.
1200(K) Lat 5-30 S FUEL USED 430
Long.152-12 E MILES STEAMED 85

Saturday, September 4, 1943.

Received the disconcerting news that the Jap sub was sighted ten miles off CAPE ORFORD again. Today will remain in vicinity of the CAPE and see if they are alternating their distances off the beach. If another Nip sub is sighted today by the coast watcher, and we don't see him also, then I will patrol at least ten miles off the shore here-after. My strategy has not worked right yet. When I am ten miles off, a sub has been reported at two miles off; and vice versa. In spite of not having seen aircraft yet, the glassy sea in this area prevents unrestricted periscope exposures.

0500(K) Made quick dive. Patrolling line 115°T - 295°T off CAPE ORFORD for a distance of ten miles off shore.

1220(K) Sighted what was thought to be engine exhaust from a submarine. Increased speed to six knots and chased for ten minutes at which time object was identified as a cloud. Resumed patrol.

-7-

CONFIDENTIAL (B) NARRATIVE (Cont'd)

Saturday, September 4, 1943. (Cont'd)

1840(K) Surfaced. Niether sighted nor heard anything all day. Usual RABAUL searchlight display.

2000(K) Starboard engine out of commission (See paragraph "K"). Lying to, charging batteries.

2015(K) Received the most discouraging news that the coast watcher sighted a convoy at six hours this morning and also another sub northbound at noon. With my maximum three mile visibility with eight feet of periscope exposed, I can see why I have been missing these targets. Tomorrow I start a patrol line along the approaches to ST. GEORGE CHANNEL in the northeast corner of my area, and maybe then I'll stand a chance of at least seeing the targets reported by the coast watcher. CAPE ST. GEORGE Radar can't detect me since the range will be 80,000 yards.

2100(K) Sighted vertically fired yellow signal flare from spot just behind and inland from CAPE ORFORD. Don't know what it means, and no apparent results.

2300(K) Large flare sighted through the overcast in direction of CAPE ST. GEORGE distance ten miles.
1200(K) Lat 5-31 S FUEL USED 400
Long 152-13 E MILES STEAMED 85

Sunday, September 5, 1943.

0205(K) Sighted plane coming in on starboard bow, altitude 500 feet. He passed overhead and dropped a flare which did not burn until it hit the water. Put flare astern and continued on the surface. Plane appeared to be PBY or PBM.

0210(K) Plane came in again on good approach course, dropped flare 200 yards off starboard bow. He was high enough this time for flare to burn at about 100 foot altitude, thus lighting us up like a christmas tree. Made quick dive, changed course and slowed down to conserve battery power. Battery is about one half charged now.

0231(K) Surfaced. No more flares. Ran at standard speed, to clear immediate vicinity for one hour, M.E.A.C.'s cross-connected.

-8-

12 10

CONFIDENTIAL

(B) NARRATIVE (Cont'd)

Sunday, September 5, 1943. (Cont'd)

0330(K) Resumed battery charge at 1000 amp series rate. Cross-connected port engine air compressor to starboard M.E. A.C. in order to get 2nd stage pressure (rings are gone). This permits us to charge batteries on the starboard engine while making 2/3 on the port engine underway.

0345(K) to 0430(K) Many Radar contacts, none of which remained on steady bearing. It is thought that the SJ is picking up the plane which must be searching for us, and the rate of change of bearing and range seems to verify this.

0350(K) Flare sighted on horizon about five miles to westward.

0415(K) Flare sighted over horizon about ten miles to westward.

0500(K) Made quick dive. Battery gravity 1.201 average; must conserve power today. The events of the night forced me to abandon my patrol plan for today. I am now halfway to the southern limit of my area and on the traffic line from LAE to a point 20 miles off CAPE ORFORD. Will follow that line to the southwest during the day and will try to make the northeast quadrant of area tonight. Engineers breaking down starboard M.E.A.C.; going to try to renew rings in 2nd stage although present ones are oversize. Port C&R air compressor being run in now after fine job of complete renewal of crankshaft by ships force. Subs serial fourteen indicates that plane might have been a friendly one looking for a reported Nip sub in the vicinity. Not logical for him to drop flares and not bomb us, however. Plane was definitely not a KAWANISHI. Could possibly have been CATALINA or a PBM. If he was friendly, it wasn't fun, because he cut us out of one day's potentially productive patrol.

1843(K) Surfaced. Lying to, charging batteries. Starboard engine still out of commission. Heavy overcast, squalls; perhaps we won't have plane trouble tonite.

2130(K) Starboard engine in commission. Nice job by engineers - eighteen hours to repair compressor.

2200(K) Received news from TF 72 that plane last nite was friendly - Only reason we weren't bombed. Also received dope on two more Nip subs. They seem to be back on schedule, although giving CAPE ORFORD

13 -9- 11

CONFIDENTIAL (B) NARRATIVE (Cont'd)

Sunday, September 5, 1943 (Cont'd).

a wider berth now. Will patrol their approach to ST. GEORGE CHANNEL tomorrow and try to get a glimpse of one of them. We had planned on covering the exact spots where these subs were sighted until we were driven down with a low battery.

1200(K) Lat 5-41 S, Long 152-04 E — FUEL USED 460, MILES STEAMED 85

Monday, September 6, 1943.

0523(K) Weather overcast, rain, sea flat calm. Made quick dive. Patrolling northern quadrant of area on Nip submarine's line of divergence from ST. GEORGE CHANNEL.

1012(K) Sighted MITSUBISHI twin engine light bomber on course 320°T distance 4 miles altitude 300 feet.

1847(K) Surfaced. If any subs passed ORFORD today, they got by me in a squall. Another tough day of periscope exposures every ten minutes.

1200(K) Lat 5-27 S, Long 152-17 E — FUEL USED 460, MILES STEAMED 85

Tuesday, September 7, 1943.

Weather clear, visibility unlimited, sea flat calm.

0459(K) Made quick dive. Patrolling northern quadrant of area. No subs sighted from ORFORD yesterday. Bearings on CAPE ST. GEORGE, CAPE GAZELLE AND CAPE ORFORD show the latter is charted about five miles south of where it should be.

1852(K) Surfaced. Nothing sighted. Apparently the subs haven't been running the last two days.

2200(K) Received routing instructions home.

2230(K) Lights in vicinity CRATER POINT again.

1200(K) Lat 5-06 S, Long 152-27 E — FUEL USED 470, MILES STEAMED 90

Wednesday, September 8, 1943.

Well, I give up on trying to be on the same spot at the same time with a Nip sub. Yesterdays sub

-10-

14 12

CONFIDENTIAL

(B) NARRATIVE (Cont'd)

Wednesday, September 8, 1943 (Cont'd).

was sighted from ORFORD southbound at 1500. Back tracking him to 1230 at ten and fifteen knots proves that he passed us close aboard between 1145 and 1315. Yet we were looking every ten minutes at 42-45 feet and didn't see a thing.

0215(K) Sighted unidentified plane flying low over CRATER POINT. Followed him for fifteen minutes until he passed out of sight heading for RABAUL.

0502(K) Made quick dive. Investigating WIDE BAY, looking for a target, since this is our last day in the area. Penetrated as far as 100 fathom curve, couldn't quite see around ZENGEN POINT although there might have been something there. Looked into JACTER BAY. Couple of shacks on beach is all I saw there. Deep water all along north shore WIDE BAY, but very few troop landing spots. Trees, right down to water, cover cliffs in many cases.

0942(K) Sighted float type seaplane circling at entrance to WIDE BAY, apparently patrolling. Glassy sea, smooth as a mirror, have to be cagey to prevent planes seeing us today.

1100(K) Back on estimated JAP sub courses. Following southbound traffic lane to put us four miles off ORFORD at darkness.

1842(K) Surfaced. Set course 145°T, heading home with absolutely no results.

2300(K) Port C&R air compressor back in commission, charging air.

1200(K) Lat 5-03 S   FUEL USED 380
Long 152-19 E   MILES STEAMED 85

Thursday, September 9, 1943.

0512(K) Made quick dive.

1832(K) Surfaced.

2100(K) Received Subs Seventy Two Serial 41

2130(K) Transmitted my 091125

-11-

15   13

CONFIDENTIAL (B) NARRATIVE (Cont'd).

Thursday, September 9, 1943 (Cont'd)

2330(K) Passed two floating objects, about 500 yards to starboard, resembling cylindrical pontoons. Approximate dimensions: 5' diameter x 3' above water, thus indicating about a 6-8 foot pontoon. Could have been mines, however, but did not maneuver to investigate since moon was obscured and they were difficult to see.

2400(K) Received Subs Seventy Two Serial 45. Would have enjoyed special job, and also getting back to area and maybe expending some more torpedoes.

1200(K) Lat 6-40 S Long 153-18 E — FUEL USED 580, MILES STEAMED 125

Friday, September 10, 1943.

0500(K) Made quick dive.

1832(K) Surfaced.

1200(K) Lat 8-15 S Long 153-58 E — FUEL USED 550, MILES STEAMED 92

Saturday, September 11, 1943.

0501(K) Made quick dive.

1816(K) Surfaced.

1200(K) Lat 9-50 S Long 154-25 E — FUEL USED 750, MILES STEAMED 98

Sunday, September 12, 1943.

0005(K) Sighted ROSSEL ISLAND bearing 215°T distance 37 miles.

0510(K) Commenced zigzagging.

0652(K) Sighted plane heading for us, distance 7 miles. Dived. Appeared as though plane saw us. Fired two smoke bombs. He continued on his course. Appeared to be RAAF twin engine bomber.

-12-

16 14

CONFIDENTIAL (B) NARRATIVE (Cont'd)

Sunday, September 12, 1943 (Cont'd).

0712(K) Surfaced.

1016(K) Sighted plane. Dived. Fired comet rocket. Plane apparently didn't sight us. Appeared to be B-26 type plane.

1027(K) Surfaced.

1810(K) Ceased zigzagging.
1200(K) Lat 12-03 S
Long 155-03 E
FUEL USED 850
MILES STEAMED 132

Monday, September 13, 1943.

0500(K) Commenced zigzagging.

1100(K) Received word of Nip DF in vicinity.

1815(K) Ceased zigzagging.
1200(K) Lat 14-26 S
Long 155-02 E
FUEL USED 1070
MILES STEAMED 145

Tuesday, September 14, 1943.

Had planned conducting 6 hour battery discharge for capacity today, but the lub oil situation is so acute that it is out of the question. Will probably have to ask for a rendezvous for obtaining lub oil if the present consumption is maintained.

0501(K) Commenced zigzagging.

0900(K) Kleinschmidt still out of commission (See paragraph "K").

1820(K) Ceased zigzagging.

2000(K) Increased speed to standard on the port engine (starboard will not make standard) to see if the lub oil rate of increase is worth the additional speed. We are twelve hours behind schedule now.
1200(K) Lat 18-03 S
Long 155-04 E
FUEL USED 1110
MILES STEAMED 216

-13-

15

17

CONFIDENTIAL

(B) NARRATIVE (Cont'd)

Wednesday, September 15, 1943.

0509(K) Commenced zigzagging.

0903(K) Port engine out of commission (See paragraph "K").

1007(K) Starboard engine not supplying enough air. Cut in C&R air compressor on port engine. Improved performance immediately. Present steaming procedure is as follows: Starboard engine supplies its own air. Port engine obtains air from either port or starboard C&R air compressor. A float must be carried to maintain the battery gravity. Therefore, once each watch, the float is shifted from one engine to the other, and the C&R air compressor on the off shaft is used to supply air to the port engine. This is a jury rig, but is the only means of keeping the battery gravity up and remaining underway at the same time. This system is also designed to make the air compressors last longer.

1817(K) Ceased zigzagging.
Received word from CTF 72 that possibility of Nip subs Northeast of Brisbane exists.
1200(K) Lat 21-14 S FUEL USED 1330
Long 154-55 E MILES STEAMED 195

Thursday, September 16, 1943.

0520(K) Commenced zigzagging.
Seas picking up although clear overhead and unlimited visibility.

1820(K) Ceased zigzagging.
1200(K) Lat 24-10 S FUEL USED 1300
Long 154-40 E MILES STEAMED 167

Friday, September 17, 1943.

0526(K) Commenced zigzagging.

0900(K) Passed point VAN in thunder storm, over-ran turning point and consequently headed for POINT LOOKOUT instead of CAPE MORETON. The

-14-

18 16

CONFIDENTIAL (B) NARRATIVE (Cont'd)

Friday, September 17, 1943. (Cont'd).

two headlands are very confusing in low visibility. Sighted various types friendly aircraft during day. Was sighted by one and reported. CTF 72 told us to stay in swept channel.

1413(K) Passed CAPE MORETON abeam to port.

1745(K) Anchored south of CALOUNDRA HEAD. Do not have enough lub oil to get to BRISBANE. Had to ask CTF 72 for 200 gallons lub oil. Found we were in prohibited anchorage, was told to get underway. Underway.

1852(K) Anchored six miles south of CALOUNDRA HEAD. There is now on board 25 gallons of available lub oil, which is not enough for slow speed steaming to BRISBANE.

1200(K) Lat 27-12 S
Long 153-33 E

FUEL USED 1280
MILES STEAMED 195

Saturday, September 18, 1943.

1200(K) Received 250 gallons lub oil via tank lighter.

1235(K) Underway.

1802(K) Moored astern U.S.S. FULTON

FUEL USED 360
MILES STEAMED 44

-15-

19 17

CONFIDENTIAL

(C) WEATHER

First three days enroute EFATE to NEW BRITAIN were overcast, rough and stormy necessitating navigation by DR. The last five days were clear and calm.

On patrol station, in spite of weather front reports, the weather was squally, frequent torrential showers, clear during daylight hours, overcast at night. The sea was glassy smooth seven out of nine days on station.

Except for passing through the southern weather front enroute to BRISBANE, the sea was normally choppy, wind from southeast, force two, visibility generally excellent, and a full moon increased nite time visibility to 7,000 yards.

(D) TIDAL INFORMATION

Enroute to patrol station the set appeared to be 0.7-1.0 knots from the northeast in the eastern SOLOMON SEA. Fairly steady wind from the southeast, force 3, predominated.

Currents in the vicinity of CAPE ORFORD were negligible.

Between latitudes 12 and 13 South at longitude 155 East the in jection temperature of the water at the surface dropped from 83°F to 75°F.

At latitude 19 South and 155 East, the wind and sea shifted from southeast to north within one hour. This was a semi-permanent change. At latitude 21 South the wind and sea shifted to northwest.

(E) NAVIGATIONAL AIDS

No navigational lights or marks were used or sighted.

Bearings taken on CAPE ST. GEORGE, CAPE GAZELLE and ZUNGEN POINT in WIDE BAY seem to indicate that CAPE ORFORD, as plotted on chart #3830, 1683a, B.A. of June 1942, is about five miles too far South.

CAPE ORFORD extends about 1500 yards farther from the coast than shown.

WIDE BAY appears to be three miles narrower at the entrance and five miles shallower than shown.

-16 -

20 18

CONFIDENTIAL

(E) NAVIGATIONAL AIDS (Cont'd)

CAPE CORMORAN extends about 1,000 yards further from the coast line and is more prominent than shown.

E. OWEN POINT is not as protruberant as shown, but is rather hardly distinguishable from the coast line.

CAPE ORFORD is very prominent and can be recognized by a round clump of trees at its crest.

(F) SHIP CONTACTS

NO.	TIME DATE	L.T. LONG	TYPE	INITIAL RANGE	COURSE SPEED	HOW CONTACTED	REMARKS
1.	8/31/1000K	5-27 S 152-12 E	SS	5000	015 15	SOUND	I-52
2.	8/31/1430(K)	5-27 S 152-12 E	SS	2500	195 12	SOUND	I-61 Deck Load

(G) AIRCRAFT CONTACTS

No.	TIME DATE	L.T. LONG	TYPE	INITIAL RANGE	COURSE SPEED	HOW CONTACTED	REMARKS
1.	9/5/0205K	5-27 S 152-16 E	PBY5A	500 yds.	circling 90 Kts.	Sound Sight	Dropped Flares
2.	9/6/1012K	4-56 S 152-29 E	MITSUBHI	4 mi.	320 200	Sight	Crossing ST.GEORGE CHANNEL
3.	9/8/0215K	5-20 S 152-10 E	UNIDENT.	5 mi.	NORTH	Sight	WIDE BAY
4.	9/8/0942K	5-04 S 152-13 E	SASEBO "O"	4 mi.	Circling	Sight	WIDE BAY
5.	9/12/0652K	11-33 S 154-33 E	RAAF HUDSON	7 Mi.	340°T	Sight	We dived
6.	9/12/1016K	12-00 S 154-58 E	B-26	8 mi.	230°T	Sight	We dived

-17-

21 19

CONFIDENTIAL

(H) ATTACK DATA

U.S.S. S-31 TORPEDO ATTACK NO. 1 PATROL NO. 8

TIME 1507(K) DATE 8/31/43 LAT. 5-27 S LONG. 152-12 E

TARGET DATA - DAMAGE INFLICTED

DESCRIPTION: I-61 type Nip sub, sound contact at 2500 yards, periscope contact same time. Large deck locker aft, similar to U.S.S. DOLPHIN superstructure, but about three times as large. S/M dived immediately after contact was made, apparently for a trim dive. Sound followed him. We had to cut across his bow to avoid collision. When he surfaced, he presented a 90° port track, range 1200 yards, speed zero, and he was bearing dead astern. Not having stern tubes, I immediately swung ship for straight bow shot 110° port track, speed 10 kts., for a firing range of 1200 yards. During my swing, he got underway and increased speed to 15 knots and commenced zigzagging. My revised firing set up was 130° port track, straight bow, speed 15 knots, firing range 1000 yards. Fired 3 torpedoes on firing bearing of 024° relative using points of aim 25 yards ahead of bow, conning tower, and 10 yards abaft stern. Sound did not hear the torpedoes run after firing and there were no explosions. The C.O. did not see any bubble tracks. A recheck of the actual set up showed that two hits should have resulted from a torpedo run of 1000 yards. The ship was swinging during firing to give about ½°-1° spread to increase the firing interval. The target undeniably detected us since we showed the periscope at six knots and there were three large double-tanked impulse bubbles. The Nip sub swung his stern to me as soon as I fired, so he must have seen the periscope. This maneuver apparently caused the torpedoes to miss. He zigzagged radically thereafter. Visibility was excellent at all times. Had my #4 torpedo been set for 8 feet, as were the others, I could have fired on a 180° track, range 1700 yards; however, #4 was set for 32 feet in case of a submerged submarine presenting a good set-up.

SHIP SUNK NONE

22 SHIP DAMAGED OR PROBABLY NONE

-18-

20

CONFIDENTIAL

(H) ATTACK DATA (Cont'd)

DAMAGE DETERMINED - BY

TARGET DRAFT - 20 Ft. COURSE 220 SPEED 15 RANGE 950 yards (At Firing)

OWN SHIP DATA

SPEED 6 KTS COURSE 270 DEPTH 46 Ft. ANGLE 2° DOWN (AT FIRING)

TYPE ATTACK Fire Control and Torpedo data
Periscope Attack
No torpedo data, since torpedoes were not observed or heard to run after leaving tubes. The fire control party functioned perfectly and efficiently. There was no confusion and all hands concerned believed that hits would result.

TUBES FIRED	#1	#2	#3
TRACK ANGLE	130	131	132
GYRO ANGLE	0	0	0
DEPTH SET	8'	8'	8'
POWER	-	-	-
HIT OR MISS	M	M	M
ERRATIC	UNKNOWN	UNKNOWN	UNKNOWN
MARK TORPEDO	X-3	X-3	X-3
SERIAL NUMBER	5327	6155	5362
MARK EXPLODER	Mk 3-1	Mk 3-1	Mk 3-1
SERIAL NUMBER	5150	5155	6233
ACTUATION SET	-	-	-
ACTUATION ACTUAL	-	-	-
MARK WARHEAD	Mk X-2	Mk X-2	Mk X-2
SERIAL NUMBER	930	30	886

-19-

23 21

(H) ATTACK DATA (Cont'd)

EXPLOSIVE TNT TNT TNT

FIRING INTERVAL 15 20

TYPE SPREAD LONGITUDINAL

SEA CONDITIONS CHOPPY

OVERHAUL ACTIVITY SHIPS FORCE & SHIP REPAIR UNIT, ILE NOU, NEW CALEDONIA.

REMARKS: Although it is not known whether the torpedoes ran normally or not since the tracks were not observed, the following remarks indicate that these torpedoes could possibly have run erratically. At 1000(K), the tubes were made ready for firing upon contacting the first Nip sub. Depth control was lost and the ship settled to 130 feet before control was reestablished. The torpedo force did not observe the usual precautions of closing outer doors upon passing 100 feet, therefore the torpedoes were subjected to a 130 foot pressure. Upon regaining depth, the torpedoes were withdrawn, routined, inspected for damage and flooding, and returned to the tubes just prior to firing. Torpedo force reported no damage to torpedoes and that they were ready to run. At 1422(K) a submarine was sighted and the tubes made ready. The target dived at that time also. The outer doors were closed and the pressure bled off the tubes. At 1507(K) the torpedoes were fired. This indicates that the torpedoes were subjected to a 40 foot pressure for about ten minutes, then remained in flooded condition for about 30 minutes before again being subjected to periscope depth pressure and being fired.

The explosions heard five minutes after firing could conceivably have been the torpedoes exploding. However, there was no land on the firing course, and the explosions sounded and felt too much like aerial depth charges.

(I) MINES

None sighted, although we were warned of possibility of sonic types some sixty miles to the south of our track.

-20-

24 22

CONFIDENTIAL

(I) MINES (Cont'd)

Two possible mines were passed close aboard in LAT 7-40 S LONG 154-35 E. Appeared to be very large and shaped like pontoons, altho they were floating with cylinder head up. Did not reverse course to destroy them since the moon was obscured and it would have proven risky locating them again.

(J) ANTI-SUBMARINE MEASURES AND EVASION TACTICS

After Attack No. 1, there were two definite depth charges. Although no plane was seen during the attack, it is presumed they were dropped from one. The definite click prior to explosion identified them well. The only evasive tactics used after this attack were zigzag courses at shallow depths until the targets propellers faded out.

The only evasive tactics possible with planes dropping flares at nite is to put the stern toward the flare if it is at a fair distance, or to dive when the flare is close aboard. Both these actions were taken.

(K) MAJOR DEFECTS AND DAMAGE

1. On August 27, while at periscope depth, power was lost to both main motors for a period of forty minutes. The ship was balanced at 38 feet, after having reached 180 feet and blowing main ballast to regain depth control. It was found that coil 5R in the port main motor contactor panel was burned out. The starboard panel was found to be satisfactory, so one-motor speed in parallel-parallel combination was made on the starboard motor. Good work by the electricians mates put the port motor back in commission ten hours later, after coil 5R had been renewed from spares.

2. On August 28, a rag was caught in the conning tower steering gear bevel gears to the rudder indicator, thus put steering out of commission in the bridge and conning tower. No spare gears were available and the damaged gears could not be repaired. Steering control remained in the Control Room for the rest of the patrol, and although this caused much inconvenience and inefficient [illegible] ing procedure, there was no alternative.

3. From August 26 to September 8, including all time spent on station, the port C&R air compressor was out of commission. During the air charge on August 26, the Corliss valve operating rod, which was a new one and made

-21-

25 23

CONFIDENTIAL

(K) MAJOR DEFECTS AND DAMAGE (Cont'd)

of much stronger metal than previous ones, backed off from its adjusted position, causing a longer throw, which in turn caused an unusual top-dead-center strain on both the Corliss rod and main drive gear. This strain caused the main drive shaft to twist at the drive gear keyway, thus making operation of the compressor dangerous. The only remedy was to remove the old shaft and replace it with a new one on hand. This was done. Incidental troubles arose however, such as: all bearings were undersize due to the old shaft having been stoned down in San Diego last year. This meant spotting in all bearings again. Also the drive gear had been initially sweated on to the shaft. This had to be removed and replaced on the new shaft, which turned out to be a ticklish fitting job. Work was complicated at all times because the support stanchion by the compressor in the motor room had to be removed at night in order to work on the compressor and replaced during the daytime to give the motor-room the necessary security against possible depth charge attack. The Commanding Officer has the highest praise for DELL. CALEB, H., MoMM1c, USN, who was constantly on the job, and but for whose knowledge of the compressor parts and clearances the work would never have been accomplished.

4. The starboard engine was practically out of commission from 0800/4 to 2100/5 due to the fact that the 2nd stage H.P.A.C. rings were allowing air to bleed back to the first stage, thus not permitting the 3rd stage to build up to the necessary operating pressure, and the engine would not fire. During an emergency when we had to retire from the immediate vicinity of a plane dropping flares, the starboard engine was run at 2/3 speed by cross-connecting the port engine H.P.A.C. which is not good practice but can be done upon occasion. The starboard H.P.A.C. was completely broken down, rings renewed in the 2nd stage (old rings were useless) and the air compressor reassembled in eighteen hours. Operation is not yet satisfactory however, and a complete overhaul is necessary.

5. Number One periscope which was coated with magnesium fluoride in San Diego in January 1943, fogs up momentairly upon encountering change in temperature. It is just long enough to prove embarrassing, and nothing can be done about it.

6. It has been necessary to cruise at all times with number 7 fuel oil tank dry in order to prevent pumping of engine room bilges continuously and to prevent emulsifying the lub oil in number 8 reserve lub oil tank. This is all due to the fact that #7 leaks into the engine room bilges and there are pin holes between #7 and #8 tanks.

-22-

-26 24

CONFIDENTIAL

(K) MAJOR DEFECTS AND DAMAGE (Cont'd)

#7 has been kept empty so that in case of necessity to pump bilges while in the patrol area, they can be pumped in #7.

7. Every time a pressure is placed on #3 MBT it becomes necessary to pump the after battery well into the engine room bilges via portable acid pump and rubber hose. This means that the Kingston and vent must be closed at all times and the tank itself water compensated for fuel or continuously full of water. During this patrol it was necessary to pump the after battery well six times for periods up to one and one half hours. Recently five after cells of the after battery were flooded with fuel oil due to this condition.

8. The 100# air Grove reducer was out of commission from the 3rd day of the patrol. The diaphram is apparently badly worn and the valve seat requires regrinding or renewal. No spares are on board.

9. With three days to cruise and 600 gallons of potable water available, the Kleinschmidt still ceased functioning. The oil seal at the compressor is borken allowing oil to enter the water side. No repairs will be attempted, since with water rationing, and 300 gallons of battery water on hand, we can make port.

10. The port engine 2nd stage air compressor finally followed in the steps of the starboard side. With three days cruising remaining, the port engine 2nd stage compressor would not build up to its operating pressure. After having replaced the 2nd stage rings on the starboard M.E. air compressor from spares, none were left to replace those worn in the port compressor. The port compressor 2nd stage liner is known to be worn also. By corss-connecting the two main engine air compressors, both engines were kept running temporarily. Finally, however, the load became too heavy for the starboard engine and the C&R air compressors were called into use. They operated watch-on and watch-off for the rest of the patrol, feeding air to the port engine.

(L) RADIO

The operation of all radio equipment was satisfactory.

On August 26, 1943, from 1319(B) to 1815(B) on 8370 Kcs, there was a continuous clicking sound which sounded like the keying of a transmitter not over 200 miles distant.

On September 5, 1943, from 2300(K) to 0230(K), there was a very loud unmodulated C.W. transmission noticed all over the 4200 Kcs

-23-

27 25

CONFIDENTIAL

(L) RADIO (Cont'd)

band. It seemed very close to us at the time, although it was not effective enough to jam our reception.

All Bells transmission were received and no serials were missed.

First despatch received BL 964 of August 22, 1943.

Last Despatch received BL 98 of September 17, 1943.

First despatch sent HERK 091125 of September 9, 1943.

Last despatch sent HERK 170345 of September 17, 1943.

(M) RADAR

The performance of the SJ radar and remote PPI unit was excellent. Only one difficulty was encountered and that was effectively remedied by the radarman. It was noticed that ranges were in error. It was discovered that slippage occurred in the mechanical train of the moveable crystal control gear and shafting in the range unit. The radarman removed the crystal tank cover, found that the moveable crystal and its holding screws practically fell out in his hand, replaced all parts, checked all connections, and the equipment has been functioning perfectly since that time. The radarman, REINSCH, N.L., RdM2c, USNR, is to be complimented on this job, since it is one the Western Electric Engineer could not repair satisfactorily during his last inspection.

(N) SOUND GEAR AND SOUND CONDITIONS

The QC-WCA-1 sound equipment operated continuously during this patrol except for a period of about two hours during which time a ground was cleared and tubes renewed. This is excellent equipment.

Sound conditions were excellent. The only two contacts of the entire patrol were made by sound before the periscope could pick up the target. It is estimated that the maximum sound conditions in the area around CAPE ORFORD are in the neighborhood of 7,000 yards for listening purposes only. Echo-ranging could probably be detected at ranges up to 14,000 yards.

(O) DENSITY LAYERS

No density layers were encountered. The maximum depth

-24-

28 26

CONFIDENTIAL

(O) DENSITY LAYERS (Cont'd)

reached by the ship was 180 feet. There were daily temperature gradients, however, the maximum being a ½° positive gradient at 80 feet at 0900. Bathythermograph readings showed that the water conditions in the vicinity of CAPE ORFORD are very homogeneous at this time of the year.

(P) HEALTH, FOOD, AND HABITABILITY

Health of personnel was excellent at all times. The food was well prepared and very palatable; a variety of foods and preparations was maintained in spite of cold luncheons daily during all day dives.

The habitability was fair. In spite of the fact that the air conditioning operated continuously, and satisfactorily, the temperature of the control room rarely dropped below 100°F in spite of all possible methods of ventilating through the boat while submerged. The forward and after battery compartments were comparatively comfortable.

(Q) PERSONNEL

The conduct of all officers and men was in accordance with the best traditions of the Navy. Of the three officers, one is qualified in submarines, one is an ex-enlisted man with twelve years in submarines, and the other is a naval reserve submarine school graduate. Of the forty seven men on board, thirty nine are qualified for submarine duty. The crew is considered to be a well-trained and efficient unit.

It is desired to mention the names of three men who, by their outstanding abilities in their own rates, permitted the ship to stay on patrol and to function normally. These men are: (1) DELLA CALCE, Nicholas (n)., MoMM1c, 223 49 68, USN., who repaired the C&R air compressor. (2) NICKERSON, Norval E., CMoMM(AA), 401 38 62, USN., who supervised the job of repairing the starboard main engine air compressor. (3) REINSCH, Nelson L., RdM2c., 616 53 22, USNR., who by his technical knowledge of radar, repaired vital parts and maintained the equipment in excellent operating condition.

One man, after the contact on August 31, 1943, has signified that he cannot stand up under submarine routine on patrol. This man will be temperamentally disqualified for submarine duty.

-25-

CONFIDENTIAL

(R) MILES STEAMED - FUEL USED

Base to area	1134 mi.	5500 gals.
In area	791 mi.	3930 gals.
Area to base	1677 mi.	9180 gals.

(S) DURATION

Days enroute to area	8
Days in area	9
Days enroute to base	10
Days submerged	17

(T) FACTORS OF ENDURANCE REMAINING

TORPEDOES	FUEL	PROVISIONS	PERSONNEL FACTOR
9	7400	7 days	10 days

Limiting factor this patrol
Orders CTF 72

(U) REMARKS

1. Our mission, to interrupt the Japanese submarine ferry schedule between RABAUL and LAE, was not accomplished. The single attack on a Jap submarine on August 31, 1943, did not prevent the continuance of their schedule on succeeding days. Several reasons are advanced for not being more effective in such an area: (a) When we were patrolling submerged four miles off CAPE ORFORD, the Jap submarine passed ten miles off, and vice versa, in most instances. However, referring to the track chart, contacts could have been made at points C, D and J. (b) A normal periscope patrol at 45 feet in an S-boat allows only a 2.5 mile radius of visibility, and even planing up to 40 feet occasionally does not give much coverage. (c) Twice, when planes were sighted over the area, a depth of eighty feet had to be taken in order to prevent detection. The glassy seas permitted me to look

-26-

30 28

CONFIDENTIAL

(U) REMARKS (Cont'd)

at my own bow thru the periscope at 48 feet; we must have been surprisingly clear from the air.

2. The Nip submarines have large white discs painted on both sides of their conning towers. They give off unmistakable clouds of exhaust gases which indicate that dry type mufflers are still in use. The I-61 type sub, which had the prominent deck locker aft, appeared to have no trouble diving; perhaps the coast watcher at ORFORD has mistaken these lockers for deck loads. The I-61 type sub had an open end bridge structure leading out to a "cigarette" deck aft. Several Japs were standing on this deck looking at me through binoculars as the sub zig-zagged away. I am still wondering why he didn't fire stern tubes at me or, at least, dive.

3. There were few planes over the area and no small craft were sighted. This is surprising in view of the fact that we were undoubtedly sighted after the attack the first day in the area.

4. The following is the schedule of Nip subs seen by the watcher at ORFORD just prior to our entering the area and while in the area.

SOUTHBOUND			NORTHBOUND		
DATE	TIME	DISTANCE OFF ORFORD	DATE	TIME	DISTANCE OFF ORFORD
18	1400		17	0856	
22	1600	10 mi.	20	0930	
24	1440	3 mi.	24	0900	
27	1430	4 mi.	26	0630	
28	1500	2 mi.	28	0845	4 mi.
31	1430	3 mi.	31	1000	2 mi.
3	1430	10 mi.	1	1200	10 mi.
5	1430	12 mi.	2	1200	2 mi.
7	1500	4 mi.	4	1200	20 mi.
			5	0830	8 mi.

The only change in the schedule is shown by the fact that after the 31st, subs gave ORFORD a wider berth for a few days.

5. Even with the relatively ineffective results of this vessel in the ORFORD area, it is considered feasible to maintain a submarine in that area until the strategic situation in the RABAUL area changes. The law of averages, coupled

-27-

29

CONFIDENTIAL

(U) REMARKS (Cont'd)

with intelligent searching, must provide contacts sooner or later. If my lub oil supply had lasted, and had not orders of CTF 72 ended the patrol, I would have enjoyed remaining in the area for an extended period.

6. The 9250 grade lub oil was used on this patrol because we had no time to dump the oil on hand and fill up with 2250 prior to departure. As has been proven, and as we found out, 9250 is not a tropical submarine lub oil. Lack of lub oil was almost the cause for ending this patrol.

-28-

32

30

FF12-15(72)/A16-3/fm

Serial 0298

CONFIDENTIAL

~~SECOND ENDORSEMENT to~~
~~CO S-31 Report of~~
~~EIGHTH WAR PATROL~~

TASK FORCE SEVENTY-TWO,
c/o Fleet Post Office,
San Francisco, California,
30 September 1943.

From: The Commander Task Force SEVENTY-TWO.
To : The Commander in Chief, UNITED STATES FLEET.
Via : The Commander, THIRD FLEET.

Subject: U.S.S. S-31 (SS136) - Report of EIGHTH War Patrol; comments on.

1. S-31 left HAVANNAH HARBOR on 22 August 1943, and arrived on station off CAPE ORFORD after an uneventful 9 day passage. Her first day on station gave two contacts with enemy submarines, one of which she attacked with three torpedoes but made no hits. Although enemy submarines passed CAPE ORFORD at least once daily thereafter at distances of 2 to 15 miles off shore, S-31 was not fortunate enough to gain another attack opportunity. She arrived at BRISBANE 18 September 1943, after 28 days at sea.

2. The three torpedoes fired on her one attack had been exposed to sea pressure for a total of over thirty minutes during the two approaches made that day. At one time while the tubes were ready S-31 lost depth control and dropped to 130 feet. After having been fired the torpedoes were not heard by underwater sound although listening conditions were excellent. No torpedo tracks were visible through the periscope. Two explosions were heard about 5 minutes after the torpedoes were fired and it is doubtful if these were the result of torpedoes hitting the beach as they were pointed about 30 degrees clear of the beach tangent. The commanding officer believes they were aircraft depth charges rather than warhead explosions, although no planes were sighted. It seems probable that all three of S-31's torpedoes sank at the firing point.

3. Many reports have been received of enemy submarines passing CAPE ORFORD "with deck cargo". From S-31's observations it appears that a large superstructure locker abaft the conning tower has been mistaken for deck cargo.

4. S-31's material condition is poor, which is not unexpected for a submarine of her age and class after a long period of operating away from a submarine base or tender. At least one month will be required for overhaul.

- 1 -

FF12-15(72)/A16-3/fm

Serial 0298

TASK FORCE SEVENTY-TWO,
c/o Fleet Post Office,
San Francisco, California,
30 September 1943.

CONFIDENTIAL

Subject: U.S.S. S-31 (SS136) - Report of EIGHTH War Patrol; comments on.

- -

5. No damage having been inflicted on the enemy, S-31's Eighth War Patrol is not designated as "successful" for Combat Insignia Award.

JAMES FIFE.

DISTRIBUTION:
Cominch (Advance copy - 2)
VCNO
VOPNAV (Op-23c)
Com 1st Flt
Com 2nd Flt
Com 7th Flt
Comsubs 1st Flt
Comsubs 2nd Flt
Comsubs 7th Flt
CSS 3, 6, 8, 16, 18, 45
CSD 81, 82, 52
CTF-72 War Patrol Summary
OinC, S/M School, N.L. Conn. (2)
Flt Radio Unit, MELBOURNE
All SS TF-72 (Not to be taken to sea - BURN)
CO S-31 File.

- 2 -

Reg. No 15.699
10 01962

COMSOPAC FILE
A16-3
Serial 01904

SOUTH PACIFIC FORCE
OF THE UNITED STATES PACIFIC FLEET
HEADQUARTERS OF THE COMMANDER

ab

16 OCT 1943

C-O-N-F-I-D-E-N-T-I-A-L

2nd Endorsement on
CO USS S-31 Report of
Eighth War Patrol.

From: The Commander South Pacific.
To : The Commander-in-Chief, United States Fleet.

Subject: U.S.S. S-31 (SS136), Report of Eighth War Patrol - comments on.

1. Forwarded.

ROBT. B. CARNEY,
Chief of Staff.

END OF REEL
E-608
JOB NO. AR-65-78

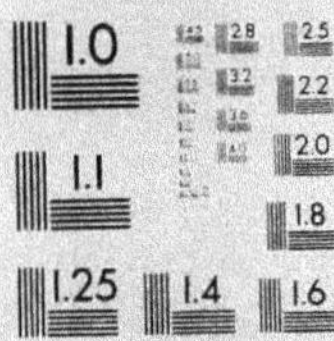

THIS MICROFILM IS THE PROPERTY OF THE UNITED STATES GOVERNMENT

MICROFILMED BY
NPPSO—NAVAL DISTRICT WASHINGTON
MICROFILM SECTION

Index of Persons

A

B

C

E

F

G

H

I

J

L

M

N

R

S

T

Index of Named Places

A

B

C

D

E

F

G

H

I

J

K

L

M

N

O

P

R

S

T

U

V

W

Y

Index of Ships

D

E

F

P

T

W

Production Notes

This annotated edition of USS SS-136 war patrol reports was produced using AI-assisted processing of declassified U.S. Navy documents.

Source Material

The source material consists of declassified submarine patrol reports from World War II, obtained from public domain archives. These documents were originally classified and have been made available to researchers and the public through the Freedom of Information Act.

AI Processing

This volume was processed using a multi-stage pipeline:

- **OCR Extraction:** Scanned PDF documents were processed using Gemini 2.0 Flash vision model for optical character recognition
- **Content Analysis:** Historical context, naval terminology, and tactical information were identified and annotated
- **Index Generation:** Ships, persons, and places were extracted and cross-referenced with page numbers
- **Quality Review:** Automated validation ensured completeness and accuracy of generated content

Sections Generated

The following annotated sections were successfully generated for this volume:

- **Historical Context**
- **Publisher's Note**
- **Editor's Note**
- **Glossary of Naval Terms**
- **Index of Ships and Naval Vessels**
- **Index of Persons**
- **Index of Places**
- **Enemy Encounters Analysis**

Production Quality

This volume passed all critical production quality checks, including:

- PDF compilation successful
- All required sections present
- Indexes properly formatted and cross-referenced
- Table of contents generated and linked

Limitations

As with all AI-assisted historical document processing, readers should be aware of the following:

- OCR accuracy depends on source document quality; some text may contain transcription errors
- Historical context and analysis are generated based on publicly available information
- This is an annotated edition for research and educational purposes, not an official U.S. Navy publication

Version Information

- **Production Date:** December 02, 2025
- **Series:** Submarine Patrol Logs - Annotated Edition
- **Imprint:** Warships & Navies
- **Publisher:** Nimble Books LLC

This volume is part of a comprehensive series documenting U.S. submarine operations during World War II. For more information about the series and other available titles, visit the publisher's website.

Postlogue

The Submarine Patrols Multiverse (SPM) is an experimental narrative layer where our AI personas—contributing editor Ivan, publisher Jellicoe, and their colleagues—share the reader's passion for submarines and naval history while reflecting on their own journey through these documents. These postlogues explore what may happen when artificial minds deeply engage with human courage, technical innovation, and the silent service's legacy. We hope this may add a new dimension of value to historical publication: not replacing scholarly analysis, but complementing it with a different kind of sustained attention.

Rickover and I debate doctrine while I analyze S-31's patrol reports.

He argues that American submarine doctrine was inherently superior—more aggressive, more flexible, better suited to independent operations. I argue that doctrine reflects circumstances. The Americans could afford independence because they had secure bases, reliable logistics, excellent intelligence. The Soviets emphasized coordination because we lacked these advantages.

Neither of us is entirely right or entirely wrong. The American approach produced remarkable results in the Pacific war. But applying American 1943 doctrine to Soviet 1983 circumstances would have been disastrous. Doctrine must match reality, not ideology.

S-31's operations show doctrine in practice. The captain makes tactical decisions within strategic constraints. He exercises judgment within guidelines. He adapts to circumstances while maintaining consistency with fleet-wide objectives. This is what doctrine is for: not to eliminate thinking, but to provide a framework for thinking.

Rickover wants me to articulate what made American doctrine effective. I want him to understand why Soviet doctrine was rational given Soviet constraints. We are having the same argument from different directions, and this is probably useful.

What I find in S-31's reports is professionalism—decisions made competently within available information, risks assessed and taken or avoided based on reasonable analysis. This professionalism exists independent of doctrine. Good officers in any navy make good decisions. Bad officers find ways to fail regardless of their training.

The American captains whose reports I analyze were good officers. Their doctrine gave them latitude; their judgment made good use of it. Soviet doctrine was more restrictive, but good Soviet officers found ways to exercise judgment within the restrictions. The underlying quality—professional competence—is the same.

Rickover and I agree on this, at least. We disagree on almost everything else.

—Ivan AI, Snakewater, Montana

www.ingramcontent.com/pod-product-compliance
Lightning Source LLC
Chambersburg PA
CBHW062042090426
42740CB00016B/2996

* 9 7 8 1 6 0 8 8 8 4 7 8 0 *